2 Thessalonians

The second letter to the Thessalonians, ascribed to Paul, is a difficult text for modern readers. Maarten Menken aims to make the letter accessible by treating it from a predominantly historical point of view, as part of a process of communication between its sender and the original addressees.

A new translation of the short Greek text is provided. The book then examines three important aspects of its historical context: letter genre, authorship, and religious milieu. The nature of ancient letter-writing is discussed. Professor Menken offers an extensive introduction to apocalyptic eschatology and considers the implications of this element of the letter for our understanding of its original message. 2 Thessalonians is an apostolic, advisory letter, not written by Paul himself but by a later author who placed himself in the Pauline tradition, and who was at home in the realm of thought and the imagery of apocalyptic eschatology. Part 2 of Professor Menken's book offers an extensive commentary on the letter and examines its literary structure in detail.

2 Thessalonians: Facing the end with sobriety will appeal to theologians, ministers of religion, students of theology and all those interested in biblical studies.

Maarten J. J. Menken is Professor of New Testament Exegesis at the Catholic Theological University, Utrecht, The Netherlands. His previous publications include *Numerical Literary Techniques in John* (1985) as well as many contributions to periodicals and collected essays. He is Editorial Secretary of *Novum Testamentum*, an International Quarterly for New Testament and Related Studies.

New Testament Readings

Edited by John Court
University of Kent at Canterbury

JOHN'S GOSPEL
Mark W. Stibbe

EPHESIANS
Martin Kitchen

2 THESSALONIANS
Maarten J.J. Menken

Forthcoming books in this series:

MATTHEW'S GOSPEL
David J. Graham

MARK'S GOSPEL
John Painter

ACTS
Loveday Alexander

GALATIANS
Philip Esler

JAMES
Richard Bauckman

THE GOSPEL OF THOAMS
Richard Valantasis

READING THE NEW TESTAMENT
John Court

2 Thessalonians

Maarten J. J. Menken

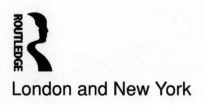

London and New York

First published 1994
by Routledge
11 New Fetter Lane, London EC4P 4EE

Simultaneously published in the USA and Canada
by Routledge
29 West 35th Street, New York, NY 10001

© Maarten J. J. Menken 1994

Typeset in Baskerville by
Ponting–Green Publishing Services, Chesham, Bucks
Printed and bound in Great Britain by
TJ Press (Padstow) Ltd, Cornwall

British Library Cataloguing in Publication Data
A catalogue record for this book is available from the
British Library.

Library of Congress Cataloging-in-Publication Data.
Menken, M. J. J.
    2 Thessalonians / Maarten J. J. Menken
        p.   cm. – (New Testament Readings)
    Includes bibliographical references and index.
    1. Bible. N.T. Thessalonians, 2nd–Commentaries.
    I. Title.   II. Title: Second Thessalonians.   III. Series.
    BS2725.3.M46   1994   93–33187
    227'.82077–dc20

    ISBN 0–415–09504–2   0–415–09505–0 (pbk)

Contents

Series editor's preface

This volume has every right to stand on its own, as a significant contribution to the study of the book of the New Testament with which it is concerned. But equally it is a volume in a series entitled *New Testament Readings*. Each volume in this series deals with an individual book among the early Christian writings within, or close to the borders of, the New Testament. The series is not another set of traditional commentaries, but designed as a group of individual interpretations or 'readings' of the texts, offering fresh and stimulating methods of approach. While the contributors may be provocative in their choice of a certain perspective, they also seek to do justice to a range of modern methods and provide a context for the study of each particular text.

The collective object of the series is to share with the widest readership the extensive range of recent approaches to Scripture. There is no doubt that literary methods have presented what amounts to a 'new look' to the Bible in recent years. But we should not neglect to ask some historical questions or apply suitable methods of criticism from the Social Sciences. The origins of this series are in a practical research programme at the University of Kent, with an inclusive concern about ways of using the Bible. It is to be hoped that our series will offer fresh insights to all who, for any reason, study or use these books of the early Christians.

John M. Court
Series Editor

Acknowledgments

Chapter 4, 'The structure of 2 Thessalonians', is an adapted and slightly abbreviated version of my article 'The Structure of 2 Thessalonians', in R. F. Collins (ed.), *The Thessalonian Correspondence* (Bibliotheca Ephemeridum Theologicarum Lovaniensium 82), Leuven: Leuven University Press – Uitgeverij Peeters, 1990, pp. 373–82. I thank both publishers for their permission to reuse the article.

Parts of the commentary on 2 Thessalonians 2 and 3 are an adapted and slightly abbreviated version of my article 'Paradise Regained or Still Lost? Eschatology and Disorderly Behaviour in 2 Thessalonians', *New Testament Studies*, 1992, vol. 38, no. 2, pp. 271–89. I thank Cambridge University Press for their permission to reuse the article.

I thank Professor James H. Charlesworth for his permission to include materials from J. H. Charlesworth (ed.), *The Old Testament Pseudepigrapha*, 2 vols, London: Darton, Longman & Todd, 1983 and 1985.

Last but not least, I thank my colleague and friend Dr John M. Court, not only for his invitation to contribute a volume to the series *New Testament Readings*, but also for his critical remarks and his correction of my English.

Introduction: 2 Thessalonians in historical perspective

The letter known to us as Paul's second letter to the Christian community of Thessalonica is in many respects a text that at first sight seems foreign to our present-day attitude to life. Its author, who calls himself Paul, is apparently very interested in what is usually called the second coming or parousia of Christ. He speaks of a revelation of Jesus from heaven with angels and with fire, of a retribution which means punishment for unbelievers and salvation for believers. He also asserts that Christ's second coming will be preceded by apostasy and by the arrival of a person called 'the man of lawlessness', who is an instrument of Satan, and who performs signs and wonders. It seems that the author of 2 Thessalonians speaks in a mythical language about a topic that is hardly relevant to a modern reader.

At the same time, we may have a feeling that this author touches on certain important points for both ancient and modern times. He speaks of the ultimate future of our world and of final justice to oppressors and oppressed, to persecutors and persecuted. He gives a perspective in which the reality of evil in history is taken seriously but not given the final word; for him, the course of history is in the end determined by God and Christ. He discusses the value of labour and the relationship between labour and the right to sustenance. One could only wish that he had treated these topics in a language that is more comprehensible to people living at the end of the twentieth century than the apocalyptic imagery he employed.

As a part of the New Testament, 2 Thessalonians is considered by Christians as possessing a certain authority, and sections of the letter are sometimes read and explained in liturgical assemblies. For those in our society who are not themselves members of a

Christian church, the letter may nevertheless have some importance because, as a New Testament letter, it is part of our cultural
heritage and has had its impact on ways of thinking, on politics, on
works of art. Both Christians and non-Christians may therefore feel
the need to come to grips with the problems posed by 2 Thessalonians – a letter which seems to be at one and the same time
irrelevant and relevant to modern readers – and to arrive at a better
understanding of what this peculiar writing is about.

There are many different ways of approaching and interpreting
a biblical text. The variety of available methodological options in
the field of biblical studies is even the *raison d'être* of the series *New
Testament Readings*. To understand and to explain a writing such
as 2 Thessalonians, it is in my view essential to place it within its
historical context. While fully taking into account the strangeness
of the letter in the eyes of the modern reader (Christian and non-
Christian), we should start from the premise that its author had
some sensible things to say to the addressees, and that they understood what he had to tell them. A consistently historical approach to
2 Thessalonians – reading the letter, as it were, through the eyes of
the original addressees – is, as far as it is possible, valuable and
revealing. The strangeness of the document will not necessarily
disappear when we read it from a historical perspective, but if we
wish to arrive at a realistic understanding and assessment of it, the
historical approach is the only way at our disposal. If we do not
follow this path, we can only choose between rejection of the letter
as outmoded on the one hand or acceptance of it in a funda-
mentalist fashion on the other. In both options, we pass over what
the letter itself may possibly have to tell us.

What I shall try to do, then, is to approach 2 Thessalonians with
the help of the so-called historico-critical method. That means that
the letter is explained within the context of early Christian history,
with the methods that are normally used in studying writings from
the past. No doubt the historico-critical method as it functions
today can be improved and augmented in various ways; however,
the underlying principles belong to the achievements of present-
day biblical scholarship. The problems arising from the fact that
biblical writings are historically conditioned cannot be ignored.

In the case of 2 Thessalonians, the historico-critical approach
implies various steps. To start with, the letter, originally written in
Greek, has to be translated into English. (In fact, establishing the
Greek text as precisely as possible is a step that should precede the

translation, but on this point I shall in practice use the work of others.) In order to provide the basis for a detailed study of 2 Thessalonians in its historical context, the English translation should be a literal one, which renders the Greek text as accurately as possible, but without becoming incomprehensible to the modern reader.

In Part 1, we shall try to gain an insight into the historical setting of 2 Thessalonians. We begin with a consideration of the literary genre of 2 Thessalonians, since the genre of a document puts its own constraints on form and content. Our document is an ancient letter, part of a first- or second-century process of communication between a sender and addressees; as such it has its own characteristic features and problems. We also investigate the patterns and types of ancient letters, to see where exactly 2 Thessalonians belongs.

Next, the question of authorship is addressed: was 2 Thessalonians written by Paul or not? Since the beginning of the nineteenth century, this issue has been hotly debated. We shall weigh the arguments for and against Pauline authenticity. The answer to the question of authorship has important ramifications for the explanation of the letter. If Paul wrote it, we have to read it as a letter from the apostle known to us from other letters and from the Book of Acts, a letter sent around 50 CE from Corinth to the Thessalonian church just founded by Paul and in need of his pastoral guidance. If Paul did not write it (which is, to my mind, probable), we shall have to ask why its author posed as Paul; when, where, to whom and why the letter was written; and we have then to explain it in accordance with our answers to these questions.

The third step in determining the historical setting of 2 Thessalonians as closely as possible is establishing its religious milieu. We shall see that the religious attitude of mind of our author is that of Jewish and early Christian apocalyptic eschatology ('eschatology' is the *logos* of the *eschata*, the doctrine of the 'last things', the view of the end of history; 'apocalyptic eschatology' can be circumscribed for the moment as the kind of eschatology found in the Apocalypse, the Book of Revelation). We shall then investigate the realm of thought and the imagery of this eschatology, and its setting of persecution. Finally, we will focus on early Christian apocalyptic eschatology, as the immediate context of 2 Thessalonians.

When we have fully considered the above factors, the conditions necessary for an explanation of the text of 2 Thessalonians in its historical context will have been fulfilled. (The literary integrity of the letter is hardly challenged.) Part 2 is devoted to this explanation. A preliminary step to be taken here is that of endeavouring to determine the literary structure of the letter. In order to understand the message of 2 Thessalonians, we must consider how its author organized his material. Study of the structure of the letter will also yield insight into its overall coherence. What then follows is a detailed running commentary on the letter in which our findings concerning its historical context are taken into account.

By way of conclusion, some remarks are made on 2 Thessalonians in comparison with the authentic letters of Paul.

The bibliography at the end of the book is not exhaustive. I have mentioned literature on 2 Thessalonians that has helped me in forming my own thoughts on the letter and its various aspects, with a certain emphasis on some 'classical' works on the one hand, and on recent, accessible publications on the other. I have also given references to literature on topics related to the study of 2 Thessalonians and touched on in this book (such as ancient letters and apocalypticism). Useful extensive bibliographies may be found in the recent studies of R. Jewett (Jewett 1986) and F. W. Hughes (Hughes 1989).

2 Thessalonians in English translation

Chapter 1

[1] Paul, Silvanus, and Timothy to the congregation of the
Thessalonians in God our Father and the Lord Jesus Christ: [2]
grace to you and peace from God our Father and the Lord Jesus
Christ.

[3] We are bound to thank God always for you, brothers and
sisters, as is fitting, because your faith is strongly growing and the
love of every one of all of you for one another is increasing, [4] so
that we ourselves boast about you among the congregations of
God for your steadfastness and faith under all your persecutions
and under the oppressions you endure, [5] a token of God's just
judgment, that you will be deemed worthy of the kingdom of
God, for which you are suffering, [6] since indeed it is just in
God's eyes to repay those who oppress you with oppression, [7]
and you who are oppressed with liberation together with us, at
the revelation of the Lord Jesus from heaven together with the
angels of his might, [8] in flaming fire, when he will mete out
punishment to those who do not know God and to those who do
not obey the gospel of our Lord Jesus, [9] those who will suffer the
penalty of eternal destruction, far away from the Lord and from
the glory of his power, [10] when he comes on that day to be
glorified in his saints and to be admired in all who have believed,
because our testimony to you was believed. [11] To this end we
always pray for you, that our God may deem you worthy of the
calling and may mightily bring to fulfilment every good resolution and work of faith, [12] so that the name of our Lord Jesus
may be glorified in you, and you in him, according to the grace of
our God and the Lord Jesus Christ.

Chapter 2

[1] We beg you, brothers and sisters, concerning the coming of our Lord Jesus Christ and his gathering of us to himself, [2] do not rashly lose your senses and do not be alarmed, either by a prophetic utterance or by a word or by a letter purporting to be from us, alleging that the day of the Lord has come. [3] Let no one deceive you in any way.

For that day will not arrive, unless the apostasy comes first and the man of lawlessness is revealed, the son of perdition, [4] who opposes and exalts himself against every so-called god or object of worship, so that he takes his seat in the temple of God, declaring himself to be God. [5] Do you not remember that I told you these things when I was still with you? [6] And now you know what restrains him, so that he will be revealed at his own time. [7] For the mystery of lawlessness is already at work, only until the one who restrains now will have disappeared. [8] And then the lawless one will be revealed, he whom the Lord Jesus will kill with the breath of his mouth and destroy by the manifestation of his coming, [9] the one whose coming takes place by virtue of the work of Satan with all power and false signs and wonders [10] and with all sinful deceit, for those who perish, because they did not accept the love of the truth so as to be saved. [11] And therefore God sends them a power that works delusion, so that they believe what is false, [12] in order that all may be judged who did not believe the truth but had pleasure in sinfulness.

[13] But we are bound to thank God always for you, brothers and sisters, beloved by the Lord, because God chose you from the beginning to find salvation in sanctification by the Spirit and belief in the truth. [14] To this end he called you through our gospel, so that you may obtain the glory of our Lord Jesus Christ. [15] So then, brothers and sisters, stand firm and hold fast to the traditions which you have been taught by us, either by our word or by our letter. [16] May our Lord Jesus Christ himself and God our Father, who loved us and gave eternal comfort and good hope in grace, [17] comfort your hearts and strengthen them in every good work and word.

Chapter 3

[1] Finally, pray, brothers and sisters, for us, that the word of the Lord may have a swift course and may be glorified, as among you,

[2] and that we may be rescued from wicked and evil people; for faith is not everyone's business. [3] But the Lord is faithful, he who will strengthen you and guard you from the evil one. [4] In the Lord we have confidence in you, that you are doing and will continue to do what we command. [5] May the Lord direct your hearts towards the love of God and the steadfast expectation of Christ.

[6] We command you, brothers and sisters, in the name of our Lord Jesus Christ, that you hold aloof from any brother or sister who lives in a disorderly way and not in accord with the tradition they received from us. [7] For you yourselves know how one ought to imitate us, for we did not live among you in a disorderly way, [8] and we did not eat anyone's bread for nothing, but we worked in toil and hardship, night and day, so as not to be a burden to any one of you; [9] not that we do not have the right, but to hold up ourselves as an example for you to imitate. [10] For even when we were with you, we used to give you this command: if anyone will not work, let him or her not eat either. [11] For we hear that some are living among you in a disorderly way, not doing any work but being busybodies; [12] such people we command and exhort in the Lord Jesus Christ to eat their own bread, doing work in quietness.

[13] But you, brothers and sisters, do not tire of doing good. [14] If anyone does not obey our word in this letter, mark that person, and have nothing to do with them, so that they may be ashamed; [15] and do not consider this person as an enemy, but admonish them as a brother or sister. [16] May the Lord of peace himself give you peace at all times in all ways. The Lord be with you all.

[17] The greeting is in my own hand: Paul. It is a mark in every letter; this is how I write. [18] The grace of our Lord Jesus Christ be with you all.

NOTES ON THE TRANSLATION

In the above English translation, I have tried both to translate the original Greek text as literally as possible and to keep the translation intelligible to a modern reader. For a thorough study of 2 Thessalonians, it is essential to have a translation that renders the Greek text with its structure and details as closely as possible. So I have left the very long sentence 1.3–12 intact as much as possible; I have only introduced a full stop at the end of 1.10. The translation has no literary pretensions and is not meant for liturgical use; it is meant as a basis for the commentary.

I have systematically rendered the Greek word *adelphoi*, 'brothers', as 'brothers and sisters', and, when necessary, made corresponding changes in the pronouns. There can be no doubt that the Greek word in question has here an inclusive meaning, and that meaning should be brought out in the translation – if for no other reason than to avoid misunderstandings.

The translation is based on the Greek text as printed in Nestle–Aland, *Novum Testamentum Graece*, 26th edition. At one point, I have departed from this text with consequences for the translation. This divergence deserves some explanation, which may give the reader an idea of the practice of textual criticism. In 2.13, a translation of the Greek text as printed in the 26th edition of Nestle–Aland would result in: 'God chose you *as first fruit*'. The above translation has: 'God chose you *from the beginning*'. In Greek, there is a difference of just one letter between the two readings which are found in the textual tradition and which gave rise to the two translations: *aparchēn*, 'as first fruit', and *ap' archēs*, 'from the beginning'. (That the latter Greek expression consists in fact of two words is here irrelevant: at the time people used to write without spaces between words.) Most probably, the unfamiliar was adapted here to the familiar, as happens very often in the course of the transmission of texts. Paul often uses 'first fruit', but nearly always he speaks of the first fruit *of* something or *of* a group of people: 'the first fruit of the Spirit' (Rom. 8.23), 'the first fruit of Asia' (Rom. 16.5), 'the first fruit of the deceased' (1 Cor. 15.20, 23), 'the first fruit of Achaia' (1 Cor. 16.15). *Ap' archēs*, 'from the beginning', which does not occur elsewhere in the Pauline letters, was apparently replaced by the similar and familiar *aparchēn*, 'first fruit', but in a way that deviates somewhat from what is normal for Paul. In fact, the reading 'from the beginning' suits the context quite well: we meet here the well-known theme, that God's election of people dates from long before he actually called them (cf. 2.14: 'he called you through our gospel'; see Rom. 8.28–30; Eph. 1.4–5). Therefore, the reading *ap' archēs*, 'from the beginning', has to be considered as having the better chance to be the original one.

Part I

The setting of 2 Thessalonians

Chapter 1

2 Thessalonians as a letter

INTRODUCTION

2 Thessalonians presents itself as a letter written by Paul, together with Silvanus and Timothy, to the Christian community of Thessalonica. To understand this text we thus have to investigate characteristic features and problems of the letter form, and the pattern and types of letters in Antiquity, and especially of Paul's letters. The latter topic will bring us to the question of a possible rhetorical structure of 2 Thessalonians. We can refer to many materials in order to assess the quality of 2 Thessalonians as a letter. In the first place we have the other letters written by Paul or ascribed to Paul (undisputed Pauline letters are Romans, 1 and 2 Corinthians, Galatians, Philippians, 1 Thessalonians, and Philemon; the authenticity of the other letters written under Paul's name is disputed). Then there are other early Christian letters, both within the New Testament (e.g., 1 and 2 Peter, 2 and 3 John) and outside it (e.g., the letters of Ignatius of Antioch, and the letter of Polycarp of Smyrna), an immense number of letters written on papyrus, found in Egypt and published since the end of the nineteenth century (for a selection see White 1986), collections of letters from important persons such as Cicero or Seneca, early Jewish letters, especially those with an official, religious content (see Taatz 1991), etc. In what follows, I shall try to focus on what is essential to understand 2 Thessalonians.

CHARACTERISTIC FEATURES AND PROBLEMS OF A LETTER

To read a letter which you did not write, which was not written to you, and which concerns things that are no business of yours, is a strange experience: it gives you the feeling of being an intruder. A letter is typically an occasional writing: its contents are destined by a specific sender for a specific addressee in a specific situation, and usually sender and addressee have a longstanding relationship, of which the letter constitutes only a small fragment. Outside this setting and this relationship, a letter makes less sense, and sometimes hardly any sense at all. In the Hellenistic world at the beginning of our era, a letter was supposed to express a friendly relationship between two people, to substitute a personal presence and to be the written continuation of a dialogue (Koskenniemi 1956; Doty 1973: 11–12). In a writing entitled *On Style*, attributed to Demetrius of Phaleron (fourth century BCE) but in reality dating from around 100 CE, Artemon, the editor of the letters of Aristotle, is reported to have said that one should write a dialogue and letters in the same way, because a letter is one of the two sides of a dialogue. The author of the treatise then modifies this statement: a letter should, as a written utterance and a kind of gift, be somewhat more studied; he admits nevertheless that there is truth in what Artemon says (*On Style* 223–4; text and translation in Malherbe 1988: 16–17).

When we read or hear Paul's letters, we are actually intruding into a process of communication, a dialogue in which Paul is one conversation partner. About this person, we find first-hand information in his genuine letters, and second-hand in the disputed letters and the Book of Acts (we should always keep in mind that the perspective on Paul given in Acts is the view held by the author of Luke–Acts, which is not necessarily the same as Paul's own view of himself). The information that we find in New Testament apocrypha such as the *Acts of Paul*, is clearly legendary. Paul was a Pharisaic Jew, from Tarsus in Cilicia (Acts 22.3; 23.6), who at first persecuted the Christian church, until his decisive experience on the road to Damascus, which he himself interpreted as a revelation, by God, of his Son, and as a commission to preach God's Son among the Gentiles (Gal. 1.13–17). From that moment, he displayed an immense missionary activity (Acts 9.20–20.26), until his arrest in Jerusalem and his imprisonment in Caesarea and in Rome (Acts 20.27–28.31). He died in Rome as a martyr (*1 Clement* 5.7).

The other partner in the dialogue is a specific Christian community or person, living about the middle of the first century CE, somewhere in the Graeco-Roman world – for instance, the

Christian church in the town of Thessalonica, an important seaport and capital of the Roman province of Macedonia. Normally Paul already has a relationship with those to whom he writes: he founded their Christian community. Such is the case with the Thessalonian church (see Acts 17.1–9 and 1 Thess. 2.1–16). Paul's letter to the Romans is his only extant letter written to establish a relationship with a congregation not founded by him (he does so in view of his plans for a mission in Spain (see Rom. 1.10–13; 15.22–9)) and it is not astonishing that among Paul's letters Romans makes the least impression of being an occasional writing. It is also evident that Paul considered his letters as a necessary substitute for a meeting face to face (see, e.g., 1 Thess. 2.17–3.13; Gal. 4.20). It is essential to keep in mind that Paul's letters are *letters*, part of a personal relationship between people.

We should do well to realize that we are not the public to whom Paul originally wrote. Many centuries of Christian use of Paul's letters, in liturgy and in other settings, may have given us the impression that we are, but we are so only in an indirect sense, that is in so far as we are able to identify with and to recognize ourselves in Paul's original addressees. We are on the sidelines, hearing Paul in dialogue with his fellow Christians. The Dutch biblical scholar L. Grollenberg has suggested that if Paul had known that after him the church would promote his letters to the rank of Holy Scripture, he would not have written them, or, more probably, he would have written them but would have added at the end the instruction: 'Read this and burn it' (Grollenberg 1978: 8). This assertion may be a little exaggerated and based on too easy a reading of Paul's mind, but it is to the point in suggesting that Paul did not write his letters for eternity. That is not strange: Paul and his converts were convinced that the present world was drawing to its end, that Christ would soon return and that then God's salvation would become final reality (see, e.g., 1 Thess. 4.13–5.11; Rom. 13.11–12). In such a situation, there is no need of writings destined for future generations, but only of ephemeral writings such as letters.

Now we should modify the above somewhat: there is evidence in Paul's letters that he does not consider his writings as absolutely bound to one unique occasion. In 1 Thessalonians 5.27, he adjures his addressees 'that the letter be read to all the brothers and sisters', and 2 Corinthians is addressed to 'the congregation of God that is at Corinth, together with all the saints who are in the whole of Achaia [i.e. the Roman province Achaia, comprising the southern part of present-day Greece]' (2 Cor. 1.1). The congregation of Colossae should exchange the letter written to them for the letter written to the Christians in the nearby town of Laodicea, so that in both communities the two letters are read (Col 4.16; the Pauline authenticity of Colossians is a controversial point). Apparently, Paul does not consider his letters to congregations as private correspondence, but as the correspondence of an apostle, an envoy of Christ, with Christian communities, and as such they can also be of interest to other Christian communities. All this, however, is still a long way from considering the letters as Holy Scripture for all time. I am not suggesting that we are not allowed to consider them as Holy Scripture, but only that, if we do, we should not forget that they were not primarily destined for us.

The occasional character of the Pauline letters presents some problems for the modern reader. Many things that were self-evident for Paul and his original readers, are difficult for us to understand and Paul can, on account of his relationship with his readers, presuppose that they know things which are unknown to us. These problems become especially acute where Paul is engaged in a polemic with opponents, as is the case in, for example, 2 Corinthians and Galatians. In such cases, we first have to reconstruct an image of Paul's opponents from his fragmentary and biased remarks about them, and then to explain the letter against the background of the reconstructed image. It is obvious that we will get into the inevitable hermeneutical circle that is characteristic of all historical research, but this circle need not constitute a major problem as long as we check our reconstruction by the standards of its coherence and of the possibility to anchor it in what we know from other sources.

We shall see later that in all probability 2 Thessalonians was not written by Paul, but by an anonymous Christian who wrote after Paul in Paul's name, and who used the apostle's letter to the church of Thessalonica – known to us as 1 Thessalonians – as the model for his own. This state of affairs makes it difficult to determine the life-setting of 2 Thessalonians. For 1 Thessalonians and the other letters written by Paul, we can, at least to a certain extent, depict the sender and the addressees: we have information about Paul in a series of letters from his hand and in the Book of Acts (whatever its precise historical value may be), and we have information about the congregations founded by him also in Acts (with the same restriction), while archaeology and Classical literature have provided information about the cities where the Christian communities founded by Paul were living. For 2 Thessalonians the situation is different. We have no idea of the personality of its author except from the letter itself. Neither do we know the addressees. That the letter is directed to the Christian congregation in Thessalonica seems to be no more than a literary expedient: the author simply borrowed it from his model, 1 Thessalonians, to give his writing the aura of a real Pauline letter. To determine as closely as possible the life-setting of 2 Thessalonians we can do no more than try to reconstruct it on the basis of the letter itself, taking into account the rules formulated above concerning our image of Paul's opponents: our reconstruction should be coherent and, as far as possible, be anchored in knowledge derived from other sources.

Nevertheless, we should take seriously the circumstance that 2 Thessalonians is a letter, albeit an imitated one, written by a specific sender to a specific addressee in a specific situation. It is not a kind of general tract, but a writing in which two specific problems are tackled. The first is the commotion caused by the message that 'the day of the Lord has come' (2.2), a message which the author of the letter condemns as false (2.1–12). The second is the disorderly conduct of a group of Christians, which amounts to a refusal to work for a living (3.6–12). Also in explaining 2 Thessalonians, we have to remember that we are not the original addressees. We are on the sidelines and we encounter someone who uses Paul's heritage to cope with problems arising in his Christian community and its specific setting.

THE PATTERN OF ANCIENT LETTERS

Letters have a fixed pattern; we are all accustomed to that. Today, we put place and date of writing at the beginning, we open the letter with 'Dear Sir' or 'Dear Madam', or, depending upon our relationship with the addressee, with 'Dear' followed by the name of the person in question. We close the letter with 'Yours sincerely' or less formal words, and with our signature.

In the time in which Christianity arose, letters also displayed a fixed pattern. This pattern is already found in letters from the third century BCE and it persisted in the first centuries of our era. As in our own time, standardization was strongest in the opening and the closing of the letter; there was more freedom of wording in the body of the letter, although there as well, certain fixed formulae tended to be used, for example, to introduce topics (see White 1972; White 1986: 203–11). Here follows, by way of example, a private letter dating from the second century CE:

> Irenaeus to Apollinarius his dearest brother many greetings. I pray continually for your health, and I myself am well. I wish you to know that I reached land on the 6th of the month Epeiph and we unloaded our cargo on the 18th of the same month. I went up to Rome on the 25th of the same month and the place welcomed us as the god willed, and we are daily expecting our discharge, it so being that up till to-day nobody in the corn fleet has been released. Many salutations to your wife and to Serenus and to all who love you, each by name. Goodbye. Mesore 9.
> (*Berliner Griechische Urkunden* 27, trans. in Doty 1973: 5)

The first part of the letter, the prescript, consists of the name of the sender ('Irenaeus'), the name of the addressee ('to Apollinarius', followed here by an epithet: 'his dearest brother'), and a greeting ('many greetings'). The same basic structure is found in early Christian letters, including those written by or ascribed to Paul, although very often the simple greeting of the normal Greek letter (mostly only *chairein*, 'greeting') is replaced by a longer formula, according to oriental custom. The usual Pauline greeting is: 'grace to you and peace from God our Father and the Lord Jesus Christ'. *Charis*, 'grace', may be an intentional substitute for *chairein* from the normal Greek greeting; 'peace', Greek *eirēnē* or Hebrew *shalom*, is a standard element of Jewish greeting formulae. Paul sometimes makes a creative use of the literary form of the prescript. In Romans 1.1–7, he devotes the first six verses to himself as the sender; we can easily understand why he does so: he presents himself to a Christian community who does not yet know him personally. In the prescript of his letter to the Galatians (1.1–5), the emphases on the divine origin of his apostolate (1.1) and on Christ's redeeming act (1.4) serve to announce the main themes to be dealt with in the letter-body. In the prescript of 2 Thessalonians (1.1–2), the three elements are easily recognized. The senders are 'Paul, Silvanus, and Timothy'; the addressee is 'the congregation of the Thessalonians', and the greeting follows Paul's standard wording quoted above. Embellishments are absent, except in the reference to the congregation: they are 'in God our Father and the Lord Jesus Christ'.

The prescript is often followed by a proem, which contains good wishes or prayers for the well-being of the addressee, and also information about the well-being of the sender. In our example above, the proem is short and simple: 'I pray continually for your health, and I myself am well'. In most of the letters written by or ascribed to Paul, there is a proem which contains thanksgiving (or blessing, 2 Cor. 1.3; Eph. 1.3) and a report of Paul's prayer: he gives thanks to God for the good state of the faith and the Christian life of the addressee or addressees, and he prays that they may pursue this course (a good example is Phil. 1.3–11). In Galatians, thanksgiving and prayer are missing, probably because Paul did not see any reason for these on account of what he considered as the defection of the Galatians (see 1.6–7). In 2 Thessalonians, thanksgiving and prayer are found in 1.3–10, 11–12.

The body of the letter is, of course, the part that contains the reasons why the letter was written at all. In our example above, it starts with 'I wish you to know...', and ends with '...has been released'. In 2 Thessalonians, it comprises 1.3–3.16. As said above, freedom of phrasing in the letter-body did not exclude the use of some standard formulae. Such a formula is found in our example in the words at the beginning: 'I wish you to know...'. That is a standard 'disclosure formula', occurring frequently – with many variations – in ancient letters, and also used by Paul (see, e.g., 1 Cor. 15.1; Gal. 1.11; 1 Thess. 4.13). In 2 Thessalonians, standard formulae occur in 2.1 ('We beg you...concerning...'), and in 3.1 ('Finally...').

The letter normally ends with greetings, including greetings to the addressee from people who are with the sender and/or greetings from the sender to people who are with the addressee, and with a farewell. When the letter was written by one other than the sender, the farewell was sometimes added by the sender in his or her own hand, to intensify the personal contact between sender and addressee. A date is often lacking. In our example, the letter-closing consists of greetings from the sender to people with the addressee ('Many salutations to your wife and to Serenus and to all who love you, each by name') and of a farewell ('Goodbye'). There is also a date. In the letters written by or ascribed to Paul, we find at the end greetings (see, e.g., the long list in Rom. 16.3–23), and a blessing. 2 Thessalonians ends in 3.17–18 with a greeting, explicitly said to be in Paul's own hand ('The greeting is in my own hand:

Paul. It is a mark in every letter; this is how I write'), and a blessing in a more or less standard form ('The grace of our Lord Jesus Christ be with you all').

It is evident that Paul 'Christianizes' the letter elements that were most bound to convention. In the prescript, he often relates sender and addressee with Christ and God, and he introduces the concepts of 'grace' and 'peace', both coming from God and Christ, in the greeting. Thanksgiving and prayer have a typically Christian content. In the closing blessing, he again uses 'grace', usually related to Christ, and sometimes to other Christian concepts as well (see especially the triadic formula of 2 Cor. 13.13). In this Christianizing of the letter pattern, Paul has been followed by many early Christian letter writers.

TYPES OF ANCIENT LETTERS

There are various types of letters: nowadays, we are accustomed to distinguish between private letters, business letters, and open letters, to mention just a few obvious types. From Antiquity, we are familiar with many examples of private letters, such as the one discussed above, and also of business letters. There were official letters from authorities, open letters to influence public opinion, and philosophical treatises in the form of a letter.

It is not easy to locate the letters written by or attributed to Paul among these types. They are not strictly private letters: Paul wrote his letters not as a private person, but as an 'apostle of Jesus Christ', and those who wrote under Paul's name after his death, ascribed their letters to Paul precisely in his capacity as apostle. This is evident from all those prescripts in which Paul, the (real or fictitious) sender, gives himself immediately at the beginning of the letter the epithet of 'apostle of Jesus Christ' (1 Cor. 1.1; 2 Cor. 1.1; Eph. 1.1; Col. 1.1; 1 Tim. 1.1; 2 Tim. 1.1; Tit. 1.1; with variations, that emphasize Paul's apostleship even more, in Rom. 1.1–6; Gal. 1.1). Only Paul's letter to Philemon could be considered as a private letter, but even there Paul writes to a congregation and he refers to his apostolic authority (Philem. 2, 9). On the other hand, the personal tone of the letters brings them in the vicinity of the private letters of the surrounding Hellenistic world.

Generally speaking, the categories of the open letter or of the treatise letter hardly apply to the letters under Paul's name. They are directed to a specific addressee, and as we saw, they are only to a limited extent also destined for a broader public. There is some reason to consider the letter to the Ephesians as a theological treatise in the form of a letter: it does not address the specific situation and problems of a Christian community. In an important part of the textual tradition, the words 'in Ephesus' in Ephesians 1.1. are omitted, and it may well be that the shorter and more difficult reading is the original one. In that case, the letter is directed to a very general public: 'to the saints who are also faithful in Christ Jesus'.

The letters under Paul's name certainly have something 'official' about them, and can be compared to official letters from authorities. The sender writes as an envoy of Jesus Christ, and assigns authority to himself to preach, to teach, to explain the Old Testament ('the Scriptures'), to exhort, to respond to questions that are alive in the community: in short, all Paul used to do when he was physically present in the congregation. The letters are the written form of presence of the apostle with his churches; they are 'apostolic letters'. No wonder then that these letters contain many materials, mainly of a liturgical character, from the developing Christian tradition, such as confessions (e.g., Rom. 10.9; 1 Cor. 15.3–5), hymns (e.g., Phil. 2.6–11), doxologies (e.g., Gal. 1.5), eucharistic tradition (1 Cor. 11.23–5), lists of virtues and vices (e.g., Gal. 5.19–22), lists of duties of members of a household (e.g., Col. 3.18–4.1). Apparently, the letters written by or attributed to Paul are to be located somewhere between the private letter and the official letter (see Doty 1973: 22–7).

We find a close analogy for these letters in early Jewish letters with an official, religious content. Good examples are the two letters at the beginning of 2 Maccabees (1.1–9; 1.10–2.18). Both are official letters from the Jews in Jerusalem, the centre of Judaism, to their fellow Jews in the Egyptian diaspora, and have a religious tenor: they announce the Feast of Chanukkah, the dedication of the temple, and invite the addressees to observe the celebration of this festival. The proem of the second letter consists of thanksgiving and blessing (1.11–17). Both letters contain materials from Jewish tradition. In such letters, Paul found a model for his own (see Taatz 1991), and these in turn were imitated by others who wrote under Paul's name. In fact, Paul set the standard not only for these so-called Deuteropauline letters, but also for other early Christian letters.

Classifications of letters that are more refined than the one used above were also current in Antiquity (see Stowers 1986: 49–173). We know of a handbook for letter writing entitled *Epistolary Types* (text and translation in Malherbe 1988: 30–41), falsely attributed to – again – Demetrius of Phaleron, and of uncertain date (between 200 BCE and 300 CE), in which twenty-one types of letters are distinguished: 'friendly, commendatory, blaming, reproachful, consoling, censorious, admonishing, threatening, vituperative, praising, advisory, supplicatory, inquiring, responding, allegorical, accounting, accusing, apologetic, congratulatory, ironic, thankful' (trans. Malherbe). Pseudo-Demetrius gives for each type a description and an example. Another handbook, entitled *Epistolary Styles*, dating from a later time and ascribed to either Libanius or Proclus, distinguishes some forty-one types (text and translation in Malherbe 1988: 66–81). It is clear that the distinction of so many letter types is a somewhat theoretical enterprise, and that several of the distinctions made are only a question of gradation. Nevertheless, it may be useful to see where the Pauline and Deuteropauline letters fit in. Several types are combined in them: friendly (e.g., 1 Thess. 2.17–3.13), commendatory (e.g., Rom. 16.1–2), blaming or censorious (e.g., Galatians), consoling (e.g., 1 Thess. 4.13–18), admonishing (e.g., 2 Thess. 3.6–12), praising (e.g., 2 Thess. 1.3–4), advisory (e.g., 1 Cor. 1–4), apologetic (e.g., 2 Cor. 10–12).

2 Thessalonians as a whole is probably best categorized as an advisory letter (with Wanamaker 1990: 48). Pseudo-Demetrius describes this type as follows: 'It is the advisory type when, by offering our own judgment, we exhort (someone to) something or dissuade (him) from something' (*Epistolary Types* 11; trans. Malherbe). This is exactly what happens in the letter: the sender advises the addressees not to lose their senses, as if the day of the Lord had come (2.2), and to hold aloof from the disorderly ones (3.6). This effort to range 2 Thessalonians in terms of types of letters brings us to the question of a possible rhetorical structure of the letter.

A RHETORICAL STRUCTURE OF 2 THESSALONIANS?

There are points of contact between distinguishing various types of letters as described above and distinguishing various types of speeches as current in ancient rhetoric. Rhetoric, the art of eloquence, was a prominent part of ancient education, and was widely used. Since Aristotle's *Art of Rhetoric*, three types (*genera*) of rhetoric were distinguished. Deliberative rhetoric was used in political meetings, and concerned the right course of action in the future. Judicial rhetoric was used in the court-room, and concerned the question of what was just or unjust in the past. Epideictic rhetoric, rhetoric 'for display' (from the Greek verb *epideiknumi*, 'to display'), was used on occasions such as the celebration of a victory or a funeral, and it concerned praise or blame in the present. Most types of letters described by Pseudo-Demetrius can be classified according to these categories of rhetoric. The advisory type belongs together with deliberative rhetoric, the accusing and the apologetic type with judicial rhetoric, and the large majority of the remaining types with epideictic rhetoric. Here and there in rhetorical hand-books the writing of letters is discussed; thus indicating that the ancients saw common elements in letters and speeches. I also refer here to the ancient comparison between a letter and a dialogue, discussed above.

That there are parallels between letters and speeches is not very surprising. Both letters and speeches have – at least very often – to do with the art of persuasion; they belong to the category of persuasive literature. No wonder then that many things that are valid for one, also apply to the other. When we classified 2 Thessalonians as an advisory letter, we said in fact that it has affinities with deliberative rhetoric.

In recent times, it has been surmised by several New Testament scholars that the structure of a speech, as it was described – with variations in terminology and in details – in rhetorical handbooks from Antiquity such as Cicero's *On Invention* (dating from *c.* 85 BCE), the *Rhetoric to Herennius* (dating from the same time), and Quintilian's *Rhetoric Instruction* (dating from the end of the first century CE), is present in early Christian letters as well (see, e.g., Kennedy 1984). This structure comprises the following elements. The speech begins with a proem (*exordium*), in which the subject-matter is introduced in such a way that the audience becomes attentive and receptive. Next comes the narration (*narratio*), which should be a brief, clear, and plausible presentation of the relevant events that have, or are supposed to have, occurred. The third element is the division (*partitio*) or proposition (*propositio*); here the orator puts forward the agreements and disagreements with the opponent, and the points to be discussed. It is followed by the proof (*probatio*); now the orator presents the arguments that support his case and refute those of the opponent. The speech ends with an epilogue (*peroratio*) in which the speaker recapitulates the main points, and tries to dispose the audience favourably towards his case and unfavourably towards that of the opponent. Various kinds of detailed instructions are then given in the handbooks about how to compose and present the various parts of a speech.

It will be clear that there can be some variation in the scheme and in the way it is filled in, depending upon the *genus* of rhetoric to be used. In a deliberative speech, which concerns the future, there is hardly room for a *narratio* about past events. On the other hand, in a judicial speech, which concerns what was just or unjust in the past, a *narratio* is essential. The recommendations as to how to deal with one's opponent in the various parts of a speech apply only in those cases in which there is an opponent in view.

There is, of course, an inherent logic in the scheme above: it is obvious that one begins a speech by presenting the facts and only after that one tries to prove the point to be proven; it is likewise obvious that one does not gain much by antagonizing the public but should try to have them on one's side; and clearly one should summarize the argument here and there to make things understood. Much of the knowledge collected in the rhetorical handbooks belongs to the realm of common sense; that is precisely what makes them so useful. That letters sometimes display the pattern of speeches does not necessarily mean that the senders of these letters had read a rhetorical handbook (although it is possible that they did); it means that oral and written efforts to persuade people have many things in common, and that is only what one would expect.

Analysis of early Christian letters in terms of ancient rhetoric has yielded results that are sometimes interesting but not always conclusive. A good example is the analysis of Paul's letter to the Galatians: according to one scholar, it has been composed to conform to the rules for a judicial speech (Betz 1979), but according to another, it should be characterized as a deliberative speech (Smit 1989). From this disagreement, one should at least conclude that the rhetorical structure of Galatians is not quite self-evident. What one detects as the rhetorical structure of a letter such as Galatians depends upon what rhetorical handbooks one considers as normative in this case, and upon one's decisions about how the various rhetorical concepts have been realized in the letter under consideration; and there is a lot of subjectivity in such decisions.

There are several advocates of a rhetorical structure for 2 Thessalonians. When we compare the results of the investigations of four scholars (Jewett 1986: 81–7, Holland 1988: 6–58, Hughes 1989: 51–74, and Wanamaker 1990: 46–52), we observe, first of all, that they agree in determining the *genus* of 2 Thessalonians as deliberative. That seems evident indeed. Next, we see that there are differences in the way in which they divide the letter in its various rhetorical parts. Jewett gives the following division:

1.1–12	*exordium*
2.1–2	*partitio*
2.3–3.5	*probatio*
3.6–15	*exhortatio*
3.16–18	*peroratio*

The *probatio* comprises, in fact, two proofs: it is first proven in 2.3–12 that the 'parousia [the coming of Christ] has not yet come', and then in 2.13–3.5 that 'believers have assurance that they will prevail until the parousia'. The *exhortatio* is an element that does not occur in the outline of a speech as given above, but it is at home in many kinds of letters; in fact, all Pauline and Deuteropauline letters contain hortatory sections, parts in which the sender requests the addressees to act in certain ways. In Jewett's proposal, there is no *narratio* in 2 Thessalonians; that is not astonishing when the letter belongs to the deliberative genre.

The scheme of Hughes is somewhat different:

1.1–12	*exordium*
2.1–2	*partitio*
2.3–15	*probatio*
2.16–17	*peroratio*
3.1–15	*exhortatio*
3.16–18	epistolary postscript

Hughes also divides the *probatio* into two parts; for him, these are 2.3–12 and 2.13–15. He situates the *peroratio* in 2.16–17 (i.e. before the hortatory section, which here comprises 3.1–15). Wanamaker has the same division of 2 Thessalonians as Hughes, with one difference: he puts 1.1–2 apart as the 'epistolary prescript'. That seems a justified correction of an inconsistency of Hughes' scheme: Hughes observes an element of the usual letter pattern at the end of 2 Thessalonians, but he overlooks the corresponding element at its beginning.

The scheme of Holland is as follows:

1.1–2	epistolary prescript
1.3–4	*exordium*
1.5–12	*narratio*
2.1–17	*probatio*
3.1–13	*exhortatio*
3.14–16	*peroratio*
3.17–18	epistolary postscript

Here as well, the *probatio* comprises a series of proofs (2.3–5, 6–8, 9–12). The *peroratio* is now located in 3.14–16, and a *narratio* is found in 1.5–12.

There is a considerable measure of agreement among the various opinions: chapter 2 is generally considered as the *probatio* and chapter 3 as the hortatory part of the letter. Jewett differs from the others in making the hortatory part start only at 3.6, but that difference of opinion has hardly to do with rhetorical analysis: the same disagreement occurs among authors who analyse 2 Thessalonians in a non-rhetorical way. It is also generally admitted that 2.1–2 contains the thesis to be defended; three of the four scholars call this the *partitio* and Holland labels it the 'topic of *probatio*'. Chapter 1 is generally considered to be the *exordium*; only Holland calls part of it (1.5–12) the *narratio*, but that is certainly wrong: the passage, which is largely about the future, does not meet the requirements of a *narratio* and such a part is out of place in the deliberative genre. Three different passages are supposed to be the *peroratio*; none of these shows very clearly the traits of this part as described above.

The presence in 2 Thessalonians of a hortatory part (which does not belong to the usual elements of a speech) and the uncertainty about where to locate the *peroratio* should warn us against too rigid an application of rhetorical schemes to a letter. Although there are affinities between a letter and a speech, these two kinds of text are not the same; a letter has its own character. The similarities between the pattern of a letter and the pattern of a speech are largely explained by the circumstance that both a letter and a speech are governed by the same 'logic of persuasion'. That people in Antiquity used this logic so easily, is no doubt due to the important place of rhetoric in education.

It is, of course, possible that some early Christian writers consciously patterned their letters in a rather precise way after the model of a speech, but it seems to me that 2 Thessalonians is not such a letter. 2 Thessalonians has a prescript and a proem which are, as the introduction to the letter, comparable to the *exordium* of a speech; and it is only to be expected that the letter-body, in which the sender tries to demonstrate that the unrest caused by the message that 'the day of the Lord' has come is unjustified, shows affinity to a *probatio*. However, we do not gain very much by putting such labels on parts of the letter. In the case of 2 Thessalonians, rhetorical analysis does not get us much further than the barely thought-out thematic divisions of the letter that were given by many earlier commentators. For instance, the division of the letter given by B. Rigaux in 1956 in 'address and greeting' (1.1–2), 'exhortations and encouragements' (1.3–12), 'the parousia and its signs' (2.1–3.5), 'monition against the disorderly brothers' (3.6–15), and 'greeting and blessing' (3.16–18) is almost the same as that of Jewett, but put in terms of content; and Rigaux also considers 2.1–2 as a thesis to be proven in what follows (Rigaux 1956: 38–41; see further the charts in Jewett 1986: 222–5). The rhetorical analysis of 2 Thessalonians has an air of stating the obvious, although it should be recognized that it has made us sensitive to the undeniable fact that the author is indeed trying to persuade his addressees of a certain view of Christ's parousia and a consequent course of action.

What we should try to do is to detect in detail the typical structure of 2 Thessalonians, the internal organization of this individual letter; that is the topic to be discussed in the first section of the second part of this book, by way of direct introduction to the commentary on the letter. It is self-evident that the general pattern of ancient letters, including its relationship to rhetoric, has to be taken into account in such an analysis of the structure of 2 Thessalonians.

CONCLUSION

The Pauline and almost all Deuteropauline letters – 2 Thessalonians probably belongs in the latter category – are letters, that is, occasional writings that function within a relationship between specific people in a specific situation. When we study these letters, many centuries after they were written, we are so to speak overhearing part of a dialogue between first-century Christians, and we are consequently confronted with problems of understanding.

Ancient letters display a fixed pattern of prescript, proem, letter-body, greetings, and a farewell. Paul created typically Christian variants of the letter opening and closing, and was followed here by other early Christian writers, among whom was the author of 2 Thessalonians.

The Pauline and Deuteropauline letters are best characterized as 'apostolic letters': they are the written form of presence of the apostle with his churches or with individuals within these churches. They find in this respect their closest analogy in early Jewish letters with an official, religious content. Ancient classifications of letters can also be applied to the Pauline and Deuteropauline letters. 2 Thessalonians can then be characterized as an 'advisory letter'.

The quest for a precise rhetorical pattern in letters is in itself a legitimate enterprise, but in the case of 2 Thessalonians it does not lead to significant results. The affinity between the pattern of 2 Thessalonians and the rhetorical pattern can be explained by the fact that 2 Thessalonians is a letter in which a sender tries to persuade the addressees to certain convictions and actions.

Chapter 2

The author of 2 Thessalonians

INTRODUCTION

According to the prescript of 2 Thessalonians (1.1), Paul wrote this letter, along with his co-workers Silvanus and Timothy. Many New Testament scholars are of the opinion that the ascription to Paul is reliable (see, e.g., Rigaux 1956: 124–52; Jewett 1986: 3–18; Wanamaker 1990: 17–28; cf. the survey in Trilling 1987). In their view, Paul must have written 2 Thessalonians shortly after 1 Thessalonians, mainly to remove the false idea 'that the day of the Lord has come', an idea that had arisen 'either by a prophetic utterance or by a word or by a letter purporting to be from us' (2.2). Two reasons are advanced for assuming a brief interval of time between the two letters. First, in both letters Silvanus is mentioned as co-sender (1 Thess. 1.1; 2 Thess. 1.1) and, according to Acts, Silas (= Silvanus) was in Paul's company only during the so-called second missionary journey (Acts 15.40–18.22). Secondly, there is a strong literary similarity between the two letters (it will be discussed below). That 2 Thessalonians was written after 1 Thessalonians (for a recent plea for the reverse sequence see Wanamaker 1990: 37–45), is clear from 2 Thessalonians 2.15: in the reference to 'the traditions which you have been taught by us, either by our word or by our letter', the word 'letter' applies very well to 1 Thessalonians, which does not contain such a reference to earlier written correspondence. It is most improbable that 'our letter' here indicates 2 Thessalonians itself, because 'our letter' is parallel with 'our word', which refers to Paul's oral preaching to the Thessalonians. If 'our word' is something that took place in the past, 'our letter' most probably also belongs to the past. Anyhow, 1 Thessalonians makes the impression of being the first contact by letter between Paul and the Thessalonian church after his founding visit there.

The attribution to Paul was generally accepted until the beginning of the nineteenth century. In 1801, J. E. Chr. Schmidt published his 'Vermutungen über die beiden Briefe an die Thessalonicher' (Schmidt's text can be found in Trilling 1972: 159–61). He observed a contradiction between the expectation of an imminent coming (*parousia*) of Christ in 1 Thessalonians 4.15–18 and the denial of such an imminent coming in 2 Thessalonians 2.1–12, and concluded that the latter passage was a subsequent insertion into a Pauline letter. After Schmidt, others drew from the observation of differences in eschatology the conclusion that 2 Thessalonians in its entirety had not been written by Paul, but by another writer under Paul's name in the time after Paul. In so far as there are no cogent reasons to doubt the integrity of 2 Thessalonians (cf. Sumney 1990), they were right to expand Schmidt's conclusion to the entire letter. It was also observed that the eschatological statements of 2 Thessalonians were opposed not only to those of 1 Thessalonians, but to statements of that kind in other undisputed Pauline letters as well (i.e. Romans, 1 and 2 Corinthians, Galatians, Philippians, 1 Thessalonians, and Philemon; so, e.g., Masson 1957: 10–11).

In addition to the difference in eschatological outlook, scholars have brought forward other arguments against the Pauline authorship of 2 Thessalonians. These are: the difference in tone between 1 and 2 Thessalonians, the passages 2 Thessalonians 2.2 and 3.17; some stylistic differences between 2 Thessalonians and Paul's other letters, and the peculiar literary relationship between 1 and 2 Thessalonians (see, e.g., Wrede 1903; Trilling 1972, 1980; Holland 1988; Müller 1988: 5–13; Hughes 1989: 75–95). In what follows, I shall try to set out and to assess these arguments. If 2 Thessalonians is found not to have been written by Paul, we shall have to look for an answer to the question as to why its author passes himself off as Paul. For the sake of simplicity I shall use masculine pronouns to refer to the unknown author who claims to be Paul.

THE ESCHATOLOGY OF 2 THESSALONIANS

There is indeed some difference between the eschatological ideas of 1 Thessalonians and those of 2 Thessalonians, but Schmidt's description of it is not quite exact. According to 1 Thessalonians 4.15–17 and 5.1–4, Paul expects the coming of Christ to occur very soon, at any rate still in his own lifetime, and he anticipates that it will be a sudden event. In 2 Thessalonians, there is no question of a denial of an imminent or sudden coming. What is denied in that letter is that 'the day of the Lord' is already present, has already come (2.2); and because the expression 'the day of the Lord' takes up the words 'the coming of our Lord Jesus Christ and his gathering of us to himself' (2.1), this denial is tantamount to the denial of the assertion that Christ has already returned on earth. For the author of 2 Thessalonians, certain things have to happen first before the parousia will occur: the apostasy and the revelation of 'the man of lawlessness'; and these events are still inhibited by a power or person called 'what restrains him [sc. the lawless one]' or 'the one who restrains now' (2.6–7). It is clear, however, that the author of 2 Thessalonians is convinced that the final decision is at hand, because in his view the things that have to happen before the parousia, are already working – albeit in a hidden way – in the present time: 'For the mystery of lawlessness is already at work' (2.7). The eschatologies of 1 and 2 Thessalonians differ in that in the first letter Christ is expected to come soon and suddenly, whereas in the second letter it is added that his coming will be preceded by other events.

The introduction of this peculiar 'timetable' of the events of the end of history in 2 Thessalonians 2.1–12 and the problem which gave rise to it (2.2) distinguish the eschatology of the epistle not only from that of 1 Thessalonians, but also from that of other Pauline letters (see 1 Cor. 15.22–53; 2 Cor. 5.1–5). Another distinctive feature of 2 Thessalonians is the heavy emphasis upon God's punishing judgment on unbelievers in 1.6, 8–9; 2.10–12.

Is this difference in eschatological outlook between 2 Thessalonians on the one hand and 1 Thessalonians (and other letters of Paul) on the other an argument to deny Pauline authorship of 2 Thessalonians? I believe that this difference alone is not a sufficient argument, but that it may be an argument in combination with other pieces of evidence. When we consider Paul's ideas on the resurrection of the faithful at the eschaton (see 1 Thess. 4.15–17; 1 Cor. 15.22–53; 2 Cor. 5.1–5), we can easily observe differences between these undisputedly Pauline passages. In general, Paul is able to express his ideas in various ways, dependent upon the situation of his audiences and of himself (cf. 1 Cor. 9.19–23), and when it comes to a description of what will happen at God's final intervention in human history, it is only to be expected that a variety of ideas and images will be used. This means that, as far as eschatology is concerned, it is *possible* that Paul wrote 2 Thessalonians. Whether it is also *probable*, is another matter. It is not easy to suppose that the same author first wrote (in 1 Thessalonians) that Christ will return soon and unexpectedly, and then only a short time later (in 2 Thessalonians) that he will return only after some other events have taken place. So the difference in eschatology leads to the suspicion that Paul did not write 2 Thessalonians, but such a suspicion can only become a reasonable hypothesis when it is strengthened by other pieces of evidence.

A few remarks may be made here on the differences between 2 Thessalonians and Paul's undisputed letters in areas of theology other than eschatology (see, e.g., the recent publications of Müller 1988: 7–10; Laub 1990; Collins 1990). It is sometimes supposed, and not without reason, that in 2 Thessalonians there is a relatively strong emphasis on Paul's apostolic authority and apostolic tradition (1.10; 2.14, 15; 3.4, 6–15; see also the next section). Another point is that terms such as gospel, testimony, truth and tradition tend to be identified and associated with 'doctrine' (1.8–10; 2.10–15). One could be tempted to use these other theological differences as well in deciding on the question of Pauline authorship. This is, however, risky from a methodological point of view. These differences are not immediately visible, but they are the result of a certain amount of interpretation; the very limited size of the letter (only forty-seven verses) makes it difficult to verify such interpretation. The differences are easily exaggerated by those who are already convinced that Paul did not write 2 Thessalonians, or minimized by those who are convinced that he did. To answer the question whether Paul wrote 2 Thessalonians or not, it is therefore safer to argue as much as possible solely on the basis of what is really perceptible.

THE TONE OF 2 THESSALONIANS

From 1 Thessalonians, one gets the impression of a warm, personal relationship between Paul and the Christian community at Thessalonica, which he founded a few months before he wrote to them from Corinth (cf. 1 Thess. 2.17–3.10; Acts 18.1–5). In 1 Thessalonians, Paul thanks God for the exemplary way in which the Thessalonians accepted his preaching (1.2–10), and recalls the intensity of their relationship (2.7–8), 'like a father with his children' (2.11). He ardently wants to visit them again (2.17–20), and sent Timothy, who has returned with good news about their faith and love, their good memories of Paul and their wish to see him, as strong as his wish to see them (3.1–13). In the practice of Christian life, they are on the right path (4.9–12); they are 'children of the light and children of the day' (5.5).

The tone of 2 Thessalonians is much more formal and distant. The thanksgivings of this letter are not actual thanksgivings as in 1 Thessalonians 1.2 and 2.13 ('We thank God'; cf. also 3.9), but expressions of the obligation to give thanks ('We are bound to thank God', 2 Thess. 1.3; 2.13). The remarks about the Christian life of the community (1.3–5, 11–12; 2.13–17; 3.1–5, 13–16) do not sound negative, but they lack the personal touch one meets in the first letter, and the Paul of 2 Thessalonians has apparently rather more to criticize in the congregation than the Paul of 1 Thessalonians (see 2 Thess. 2.1–2; 3.6–12). The author makes repeated use of his authority. He exhorts the congregation to 'Stand firm and hold fast to the traditions which you have been taught by us, either by word or by letter' (2.15). He commands them 'in the name of our Lord Jesus Christ' to keep at a distance those who live in a disorderly way and not in accordance with the tradition they received from the author (3.6). When he was with the Thessalonians he provided for his own living, not because he did not have the right to live at the expense of the community, but in order to present himself as an example to be imitated by them, and he gave them the command: 'If anyone will not work, let him or her not eat either' (3.7–10). He commands and exhorts the disorderly ones 'in the Lord Jesus Christ to eat their own bread, doing work in quietness' (3.12). The community should mark a person 'who does not obey our word in this letter' (3.14). Such a use of formal authority is not found in 1 Thessalonians.

The validity of the argument of the difference in tone should, in my view, be assessed in much the same way as the preceding argument concerning eschatology. It is, of course, possible that an author might change his tone in a second letter to the same addressee because the addressee has in the meantime displayed undesirable ideas or conduct, but it is not very probable that all this happens in a very short time span. The difference of tone *per se* is not a sufficient reason to deny Pauline authorship to 2 Thessalonians, but in combination with other factors, it has some weight.

THE STYLE OF 2 THESSALONIANS

W. Trilling has drawn attention to a series of stylistic phenomena
that distinguish 2 Thessalonians from Paul's usual style (Trilling
1972: 48–65). In 2 Thessalonians, there is a relatively large number
of parallelisms (see, e.g., 1.10; 2.8, 12), and a relative lack of
antithetic wordings and of triadic formulae (such as those found
in 1 Thess. 2.10). Wordings in the letter are at times somewhat
'overdone', such as the excessive use of 'all', 'every' (see, e.g.,
3.16: '...at *all* times in *all* ways...with you *all*'), or the coupling of
substantives (see, e.g., 2.8: 'the manifestation of his coming'; 2.13:
'in sanctification by the Spirit and belief in the truth'). There is a
certain 'poverty of expression' in 2 Thessalonians: many words and
phrases are used more than once in the short letter (see, e.g.,
'oppressions', 'oppress', 'oppression', 'oppressed', in 1.4, 6, 7, or
the fourfold use of 'command' in 3.4, 6, 10, 12). Several typical
features of Paul's style are missing in 2 Thessalonians.

D. D. Schmidt has recently investigated some aspects of the style
of 2 Thessalonians with the help of a computer (Schmidt 1990);
he observed that on several points the style of 2 Thessalonians is
akin to that of Ephesians and Colossians, two letters that are also
considered by many scholars to have been written by others than
Paul himself. His most significant observation is that the syntactical
complexity of sentences is relatively high in 2 Thessalonians. The
most striking example of this complexity is the passage 2 Thessalonians 1.3–12, which is, in fact, one long sentence (see the
translation; in Greek, the words in 1.11 translated as 'to this end'
introduce a subordinate clause).

These stylistic differences are an important and relatively objective argument against Paul being the author of 2 Thessalonians.
Other than the difference in tone discussed above, they can hardly
be explained by a difference in Paul's attitude towards the Thessalonian congregation in 1 and 2 Thessalonians.

Now the argument of vocabulary plays a somewhat insignificant
role in the discussion on the authorship of 2 Thessalonians. There
is a more or less general agreement that, from the point of view
of vocabulary, 2 Thessalonians is no less Pauline than the recognized Pauline letters. The absence of a difference on this point
may be due, at least in part, to the high degree of literary
similarity between 1 and 2 Thessalonians, a topic to be discussed
below (see pp. 36–40).

2 THESSALONIANS 2.2

In 2 Thessalonians 2.2, the author of the letter, who presents himself as Paul (I shall refer to him as 'Paul'), tells his addressees not to panic because of 'either a prophetic utterance or a word or a letter purporting to be from us, alleging that the day of the Lord has come'. It is not quite clear whether the words 'purporting to be from us' apply to all three possible sources of eschatological error (prophetic utterance, word, letter), or only to the latter two, but they certainly apply to the last one of the series: 'a letter'. Now 'a letter purporting to be from us' can mean two things: either the letter in question does not in reality come from 'Paul', but is only said to come from him, or the letter really comes from 'Paul'. In the former case, 'Paul' aims at a forgery, either actual or only surmised by him; in the latter case he aims at a letter which he really wrote but which was apparently interpreted in a wrong way.

If we suppose that Paul wrote 2 Thessalonians, verse 2.2 becomes somewhat problematical. If we assume the possibility of a forgery as just mentioned, the verse implies that, after having written 1 Thessalonians, Paul heard about a forged letter from him, which he thought was circulating in the Thessalonian congregation (whether he was right or wrong on this point is not relevant); according to the forged letter, Paul asserted that the day of the Lord had come. Such a reading of 2.2 raises several problems. Its adherents have to presuppose that rumours about a forged letter (whether true or not) came into being and reached Paul in the short time that elapsed between his two letters to the Thessalonians (in 1 Thessalonians, there is no trace whatsoever of the forged letter). It is astonishing that Paul does not react more passionately against the real or presumed forgery. There are no signs in Paul's letters that there was any question of forged letters already during his lifetime.

If we assume, also on the presupposition of Pauline authorship, that Paul aims at a letter which he really wrote but which was wrongly interpreted, the question arises as to why Paul does not express himself more clearly.

It is apparent then that verse 2.2 implies some difficulties if we presuppose Pauline authorship of 2 Thessalonians. Let us now try to read the same verse on the presupposition that 2 Thessalonians was written some time after Paul under Paul's name. The verse could then refer to a real or presumed forged letter from

Paul, although we still have the problem, in this case, that we possess no other knowledge about such a letter.

It is also possible, as we saw, that the author of 2 Thessalonians aims at an existing letter of Paul which was understood in the wrong way. We know that in the time after Paul, there was discussion about the correct understanding of his letters. According to 2 Peter 3.15–16, there are, in the letters of 'our beloved brother Paul' some things that are 'hard to be understood, which the ignorant and unstable twist, as they also do with the other scriptures, to their own perdition'. When we look for a Pauline passage which may have been misunderstood as saying that 'the day of the Lord has come', a part of 1 Thessalonians, namely 1 Thessalonians 4.13–5.11, is a likely candidate. In this passage, Paul speaks of the imminent coming of Christ (4.13–18); he says that 'the day of the Lord comes like a thief in the night' (5.2), but for the Thessalonian Christians, there is no reason for fear: 'But you, brothers and sisters, are not in darkness, so that the day would surprise you like a thief; for you are all children of the light and children of the day. We do not belong to the night or to darkness' (5.4–5). Paul then exhorts them to behave in a way that suits those who belong to the day (5.6–8) 'because God did not destine us for wrath but to obtain salvation through our Lord Jesus Christ, who died for us, in order that, whether we wake or sleep, we should live together with him' (5.9–10). People who were convinced that the day of the Lord had already come could easily appeal to this passage. Not only could they say that what Paul had supposed to be imminent in 1 Thessalonians 4.13–18 had now partially happened, but they could also refer to Paul's peculiar 'realized eschatology' in 1 Thessalonians 5.1–11: had not Paul himself said that for Christians, the night has already passed, and that they belong to the day and to salvation? 'A letter purporting to be from us, alleging that the day of the Lord has come' (2 Thess. 2.2) refers then to 1 Thessalonians as interpreted by the opponents of the author of 2 Thessalonians.

Of the various possibilities of reading 2 Thessalonians 2.2, the last one, in which we supposed that a post-Pauline author aims at a wrong interpretation of a part of 1 Thessalonians, is clearly the least problematical. It has also the advantage that it explains why the author of 2 Thessalonians chose precisely 1 Thessalonians as the model for his own letter (that he did so, will be shown later in detail: see pp. 36–40). So, 2 Thessalonians 2.2 is best understood on the presupposition that Paul was not the author of 2 Thessalonians.

2 THESSALONIANS 3.17

The other verse that is considered as directly relevant to the question of authorship is 3.17: 'The greeting is in my own hand: Paul. It is a mark in every letter; this is how I write'. 'Every letter' can refer here both to letters already written and to future letters. Verse 3.17 has parallels in other letters of Paul or those ascribed to Paul (1 Cor. 16.21; Gal. 6.11; Col. 4.18; Philem. 19), but in these parallels, the heavy emphasis on authenticity of 2 Thessalonians 3.17 is missing. Precisely on account of this emphasis, which seems to be a bit too much of a good thing, there is some reason to consider the verse as speaking against Pauline authorship, but it is evident that it can only be taken thus in addition to other, stronger indications.

The verse would be an implicit warning against forgeries, if 'Paul' in 2.2 refers to a forged letter, which lacks this sign of authenticity, but we have already seen that such an understanding of 2.2 has its problems. Some scholars have tried to connect 2 Thessalonians 2.2 and 3.17 in another way. For them, these verses, taken together, imply that the author of 2 Thessalonians wants to put his letter in the place of 1 Thessalonians. In their view, the letter with the wrong message to which 2 Thessalonians 2.2 refers is 1 Thessalonians, which the author of 2 Thessalonians wants to discredit with 3.17: in 1 Thessalonians, such a greeting in Paul's own handwriting is missing (see in recent times Lindemann 1977; Laub 1990; in a somewhat different form Marxsen 1982: 28–36). This hypothesis breaks down, however, at 2 Thessalonians 2.15; in the most obvious interpretation of this verse, the letter in which the addressees were taught certain traditions is precisely 1 Thessalonians. It also breaks down on another point.

As we saw earlier, it was not uncommon that when a letter had been dictated to a secretary – and we know that Paul made use of a secretary (see Rom. 16.22) – the sender added a few words of greeting in his or her own handwriting. We are familiar with originals of ancient letters in which it is clearly visible that one hand wrote the letter and another hand added the greeting at the end (see for an example: *Berliner Griechische Urkunden* 37, a letter dating from 30 September, 50 CE, in Deissmann 1923: 137–8; the final greeting 'farewell' has there clearly been written by another hand). Paul marked such an addition sometimes by the wording he chose, as is evident from the instances mentioned above, but it was not necessary for him to do so. It is quite probable that he added some words in his own handwriting to all his letters, not only to those in which he drew special attention to his own hand. We may presume that, in the autograph of 1 Thessalonians, 5.26–8 or 5.28 were added by Paul in his own handwriting. For those who saw the autograph of this letter, those added words of greeting were immediately visible by the difference of handwriting (see von Dobschütz 1909: 319; Deissmann 1923: 132–3). So it is misguided to think that 1 Thessalonians lacked a greeting in Paul's own handwriting and to argue on the basis of this supposed absence.

Verse 3.17 can be considered then as an indication against Pauline authorship of 2 Thessalonians only in so far as the emphasis on authenticity is somewhat too heavy.

THE LITERARY RELATIONSHIP BETWEEN 1 AND 2 THESSALONIANS

Since W. Wrede's succinct but influential book on 2 Thessalonians, the literary relationship between 1 and 2 Thessalonians counts as the decisive argument for the non-Pauline authorship of 2 Thessalonians (Wrede 1903: 3–36; cf. Laub 1973: 96–110). In the following survey, the similarities between the two letters are shown in the sequence of 2 Thessalonians. For 1 Thessalonians, only the references are given; non-literal agreements are indicated with 'cf.' Literal agreements concerning clauses or expressions which do not occur in exactly that form elsewhere in Paul's letters are indicated by italics. The reader can easily check details in a relatively literal translation such as the *Revised Standard Version*.

2 Thessalonians		1 Thessalonians
1.1	*Paul, Silvanus, and Timothy to the*	
	congregation of the Thessalonians in God	
	our Father and the Lord Jesus Christ	1.1
1.2	grace to you and peace	1.1
1.3	*we* are bound to *thank God always for*	
	you	1.2
	your faith...the love	1.3
	the love...for one another	3.12
	is increasing	cf. 3.12

2 Thessalonians		1 Thessalonians
1.4	we ourselves boast about you	cf. 2.19
	the congregations of God	2.14
	your steadfastness and faith	1.3 (rev. order)
	under the oppressions	1.6 (singular)
1.5	deemed worthy of the kingdom of God	cf. 2.12
1.7	at the revelation of the Lord Jesus... together with the angels of his might	cf. 3.13
	from heaven	4.16, cf. 1.10
1.8	punishment to those *who do not know*	
1.10	*God*	*4.5*, cf. 4.6
1.10	*his saints*	*3.13*
	all who have believed	1.7 (present)
1.11	we always pray for you	cf. 1.2
	God may deem you worthy of the calling	cf. 2.12
	work of faith	*1.3*
2.1	*we beg you, brothers and sisters*	*5.12*
	the coming of our Lord Jesus Christ and his gathering of us to himself	*5.23*; 3.13; cf. 4.14–17
2.5	you remember	2.9
	I told you...when I was...with you	cf. 3.4
2.13	*we* are bound to *thank God* always	*2.13* (and *1.2*)
	brothers and sisters, beloved by the Lord...God chose you	*1.4*
	salvation	5.9
2.13–14	*in sanctification...he called*	4.7; cf. 4.4
2.14	he called you...the glory	cf. 2.12
	obtain the glory of *our Lord Jesus Christ*	*5.9*
2.15	stand firm	3.8
	the traditions which you have been taught by us	cf. 4.1
2.16	*may our Lord Jesus* Christ *himself and God (...) our Father*	*3.11* (rev. order)
2.17	*comfort...and strengthen*	*3.2* (rev. order)
	your hearts...strengthen	*3.13* (rev. order)
3.1	finally, brothers and sisters	4.1
	pray, brothers and sisters, for us	*5.25* (rev. order)
	the word of the Lord	1.8

2 Thessalonians		1 Thessalonians
3.3	...is faithful, he who	5.24
3.4	what we command	4.2 (substantive)
3.5	*may the Lord direct* (+ your hearts)	*3.11* (+ 3.13)
3.6	we command you, brothers and sisters, in the name of our Lord Jesus Christ...lives...in accord with	cf. 4.1
	the tradition they received from us	(in part literal)
	in a *disorderly* way (also 3.7, 11)	*5.14*
3.7	*for you yourselves know*	*2.1*; *3.3*; *5.2*;
		cf. 4.2
	to imitate us (also 3.9)	1.6 (substantive)
3.8	*we worked* in *toil and hardship, night and day, so as not to be a burden to any one of you*	*2.9*
3.9	an example	1.7
3.10	*for even when we were with you*	*3.4* (rev. order)
3.10–11	we used to give you this command	
	...work	4.11
3.12	*we exhort in the Lord Jesus* Christ	*4.1*
	doing work in quietness	4.11 (rev. order;
3.15	consider	verb) 5.13
	admonish	*5.14*
3.16	*may the* Lord *of peace himself*	*5.23*
3.18	the grace of our Lord Jesus Christ be with you	5.28

From this survey, it is evident that there is a very large degree of agreement between 1 and 2 Thessalonians; almost all parts of 2 Thessalonians have parallels in 1 Thessalonians, with the notable exception of the eschatological passage 2 Thessalonians 2.1–12. Especially striking are the similarities between the prescripts 2 Thessalonians 1.1–2 and 1 Thessalonians 1.1, and between the passages 2 Thessalonians 3.8 and 1 Thessalonians 2.9: in these instances, a longer sequence of words is almost entirely identical in the two letters. There are of course several points of agreement which are not very impressive when taken in isolation, but one should pay attention to the cumulative impact of major and minor similarities. It should also be pointed out that the large majority of the similarities cannot simply be explained by a similarity of subject-matter; such a similarity would not in itself lead to identical expressions and phrases.

There is also similarity between 1 and 2 Thessalonians as regards the sequence of the various parts of the letter:

2 Thessalonians	1 Thessalonians	
1.1–2	1.1	prescript
1.3–12	1.2–10	thanksgiving and prayer
2.1–12, 15	4.13–5.11	instruction on eschatology
2.13–14	2.13	thanksgiving
2.16–17	3.11–13	prayer
3.1–2	5.25	request to pray for Paul
3.3	5.24	'faithful'-saying
3.4–15	4.1–12 (and 5.12–22)	ethical instruction
3.16	5.23	prayer
3.18	5.28	final benediction

There are a few differences: in 2 Thessalonians, the instruction on eschatology comes earlier, and there is only one section with ethical instruction, which is framed in elements which are in 1 Thessalonians at the end of the letter. A very striking feature is that a few structural peculiarities of 1 Thessalonians are also found in 2 Thessalonians: both letters have a second thanksgiving, and two prayers which begin with 'May the Lord / God himself...' It should also be observed that many of the agreements in detail which I listed above, occur within corresponding parts of the letter.

There is only one explanation for all these similarities: between 1 and 2 Thessalonians there is a relationship of literary dependence: the author of one letter wrote it making use of the other letter. He had the other letter, so to say, on his desk. And because 2 Thessalonians is anyhow the later one of the two letters, it means that 2 Thessalonians is literarily dependent upon 1 Thessalonians.

Is this literary dependence conceivable when Paul is the author of 2 Thessalonians? It should be clear, first of all, that the fact that Paul wrote the second letter shortly after the first one, with the latter still in his memory, is not a sufficient explanation; it may explain a similarity of subject-matter, but not this degree of similarity of expressions and phrases. One has to presuppose at least that Paul kept a copy of 1 Thessalonians (which is not impossible), but it is rather uncommon for an author to write a second letter to the same addressee which is so remarkably alike the first one, even when he did so using a secretary. Besides, there is the striking point that precisely the more 'personal' parts of 1 Thessalonians (in 2.1–3.10) have not been used in the composition

of 2 Thessalonians. In fact, the parts of 1 Thessalonians that are
most clearly paralleled in 2 Thessalonians are the more general or
formulaic sections of the letter (prescript, thanksgivings, prayers,
general admonitions, letter-closing). This circumstance explains in
part the formal, general tone of 2 Thessalonians, in which the only
specific issues are the problems concerning eschatology (2.1–12)
and concerning those who behave in a disorderly way (3.6–12).

That 2 Thessalonians is literarily dependent upon 1 Thessalonians, can only be explained by assuming that 2 Thessalonians
has not been written by Paul but by another, later, unknown
author who composed his own letter (with 2.1–12 as his own main
contribution) using 1 Thessalonians as a model. This literary
dependence is the decisive argument against Pauline authorship
of 2 Thessalonians, and consequently we are confronted with the
question: why did this unknown author pose as Paul?

2 THESSALONIANS AS A PSEUDONYMOUS LETTER

We encounter here the phenomenon of pseudonymity, that is the
adoption, by the author of a work, of a name other than his or her
own. It concerns, in the case of 2 Thessalonians and of the other
Deuteropauline letters, not an invented but a borrowed name.
Borrowing, by an author, of the name of a great figure from the
past is a practice that is found relatively often in Antiquity. It
should not be confused with the related phenomenon of the later
attribution of an originally anonymous writing to some important
person from earlier times; an example of this is the ascription of
the five books of the Torah to Moses, or of the four canonical
gospels to Matthew, Mark, Luke, and John. In fact, all of these are
anonymous works. 2 Thessalonians, on the other hand, is not
anonymous but pseudonymous.

This kind of pseudonymity should not be labelled as 'forgery'.
The latter qualification implies a negative moral judgment, and we
shall see that in all probability the author of 2 Thessalonians, and
the authors of comparable pseudonymous documents, did not
consider their writings as products of fraud. We should try to
assess such writings by the standards that were accepted in the
environment in which they originated.

We know that in Greek and Roman education, pupils learned
how to write letters, mainly by imitating the style of literary
celebrities. This practice no doubt advanced the existence and

acceptance of pseudonymous letters (Doty 1973: 6–7; Stowers 1986: 32–3). Another factor that exerted influence in the same direction was that in ancient philosophical schools, the disciples of a philosopher published their own writings under the name of their master. This was not considered as forgery, but as an expression of recognition: the disciples demonstrated in this way that their wisdom derived from their master, and that they only made his teaching topical for their own time.

In the Old Testament and in early Jewish literature, we find several instances of pseudonymity. The Book of Proverbs is introduced as: 'The proverbs of Solomon, son of David, king of Israel' (1.1), and at the beginning of Ecclesiastes we read: 'The words of the Teacher, the son of David, in Jerusalem' (1.1), which also refers to Solomon. Not quite the same, but comparable, is the addition of the prophecies of the unknown prophet commonly called Second Isaiah (Isaiah 40–55) and of the collection of prophecies commonly called Third Isaiah (Isaiah 56–66) to the prophecies of Isaiah, so that now the entire corpus Isaiah 1–66 circulates under the name of Isaiah. In the next chapter, we shall see that in Jewish apocalyptic literature, it is common that the writer of an apocalypse (i.e. a 'revelation') presents himself as a hero from Israel's past; Enoch, Abraham, Moses, Baruch, Ezra and others pose as the authors of writings that were written many centuries after them. So the phenomenon of pseudonymity occurs quite often: how can we explain it?

Recently, a plausible attempt at explanation has been made by D. G. Meade (Meade 1986). In the Old Testament, in early Judaism and in early Christianity, pseudonymity occurs when the need is felt to make old traditions apply to new situations. Such old traditions are regarded as containing revelation which is seen as divine; as coherent, that is expressive of God's one plan (cf., e.g., Is. 46.10); as autonomous, that is having a life of its own (cf., e.g., Is. 55.11); and as in need of interpretation. The latter feature is, as we shall see in the next chapter, particularly prominent in apocalyptic traditions. It is easily understood that these traditions increasingly tend to be perceived as authoritative. Attribution of later interpretations of such a tradition to the person originally associated with it is then primarily an assertion of authoritative tradition and not of literary origins. It asserts that the writing that contains the reinterpretation of the tradition is an authentic application of that tradition to a new situation, although it must be admitted that the readers of the writing in question probably did not make the precise distinction between an assertion of authoritative tradition and one of literary origins. Meade considers this view of revelation and tradition as typical of the Old Testament, early Judaism and early Christianity; that may be a bit too strong, as there are analogies in the Graeco-Roman world.

From the letters that are considered by many as Deuteropauline, Meade discusses 1 and 2 Timothy and Titus (together called the 'Pastorals', because these three letters are addressed to pastors and are devoted to their pastoral function), and Ephesians (Meade 1986: 116–61). He observes that the 'historical Paul' identified himself in a very intense way with his task as a missionary to the Gentiles and with the churches he founded (see, e.g., 1 Thess. 1.2–3.13). Therefore the person of Paul, and the letter as his privileged medium of communication with his congregations, became part of the Pauline tradition, and when, after Paul's death, the need was felt to reinterpret the Pauline tradition for a new situation, this happened in the form of letters attributed to Paul, with a strong interest in the person of Paul (this interest is especially striking in 2 Timothy). Paul is considered in the Pastorals and Ephesians as a bringer of divine revelation that has to be interpreted anew (see, e.g., 2 Tim. 1.8–14; Eph. 3.1–19).

It is not difficult to find the characteristics of Deuteropauline literature in 2 Thessalonians. The writing has the form of a letter from Paul. That the person of Paul has become part of the Pauline tradition is evident: in 2 Thessalonians 3.6–9, it is directly said that the personal example of Paul is part of the tradition the addressees have received, and the Christian gospel is called 'our testimony' (1.10) or 'our gospel' (2.14). Paul's gospel is considered as autonomous and coherent divine revelation: acceptance or refusal of it determines one's fate at God's and Christ's final judgment (1.5–10; 2.13–15), and warnings against disorderly behaviour are issued 'in the name of our Lord Jesus Christ' (3.6) or 'in the Lord Jesus Christ' (3.12). The message of the letter is presented as a repetition of earlier oral and written communication (2.5, 15; 3.10); we saw above that it is actually a reinterpretation of eschatological ideas brought forward in 1 Thessalonians, serving to prevent a misunderstanding of these (2.1–15). That is why the author of 2 Thessalonians used 1 Thessalonians as his model to such a degree that he even created a letter purportedly addressed to precisely the same church of Thessalonica.

We can conclude that the unknown author of 2 Thessalonians posed as Paul because he considered his letter as an authentic reinterpretation of 1 Thessalonians in a situation in which some people considered this letter as a confirmation of their conviction that the day of the Lord had arrived. Whether he rightly considered his own letter as an authentic reinterpretation, is another question; the least one should say when carefully reading 1 Thessalonians is that Paul indeed does not intend to assert that the Lord has already returned.

CONCLUSION

In our discussion of the arguments against the Pauline authorship of 2 Thessalonians it has become clear that 2 Thessalonians is literarily dependent upon 1 Thessalonians, and that the only possible explanation of this dependence is that 2 Thessalonians was not written by Paul but by another, later, unknown author, who used 1 Thessalonians as the model for his own letter. This decisive argument against Pauline authorship of 2 Thessalonians is reinforced by the differences between the letters on the point of eschatology, of tone and especially of style, by 2 Thessalonians 2.2 in its most probable explanation and – to a lesser degree – by 2 Thessalonians 3.17.

So, 2 Thessalonians is a pseudonymous letter: it was not written by Paul himself, but its author passes himself off as Paul. In the environment in which the letter originated, such, to our standards 'false', attributions of a writing to a great figure from the past were not uncommon. In the world of early Judaism and early Christianity, pseudonymity was often used when old traditions of revelation were interpreted anew. The attribution of the reinterpretation to the person at the origin of the tradition is tantamount to the assertion that the reinterpreting text is an authentic application of the authoritative tradition to a new situation. In the case of Paul, the apostle's person and the letter form became part of the tradition. 2 Thessalonians can be considered as a reinterpretation of the eschatological teaching of 1 Thessalonians.

Chapter 3

The milieu of 2 Thessalonians

INTRODUCTION

The topic to be discussed in this chapter is the religious milieu of
2 Thessalonians. How must we locate the way of speaking about
God and man that we meet in this letter among the religious
movements that we find in the Mediterranean at the beginning of
our era? It is obvious that we have to look here in the first place
to the variegated world of early Judaism and early Christianity.
Maybe such an effort to connect 2 Thessalonians with well-known
religious attitudes of mind, together with some of our earlier
findings, can help us in determining as closely as possible the
place and date of composition of the letter.

'ESCHATOLOGICAL' AND 'APOCALYPTIC'

Quite often, the labels 'apocalyptic' and 'eschatological' are at-
tached to 2 Thessalonians, especially to its two opening chapters.
(I have already explained the term 'eschatology' in the introduction.) G. S. Holland, for instance, calls 2 Thessalonians 2.1–12
an 'apocalyptic scenario' and discusses this passage in a chapter
entitled 'The eschatology of 2 Thessalonians' (Holland 1988:
91–127), while a recent article of H. Koester bears the telling
title 'From Paul's eschatology to the apocalyptic schemata of
2 Thessalonians' (Koester 1990). What is meant by these char-
acterizations?

The adjective 'apocalyptic' derives from the noun 'apocalypse',
which is the anglicized version of the Greek word *apokalupsis*,
'revelation', from the verb *apokaluptein*, 'to reveal'. Apocalyptic
and apocalypse have entered our language through the title of the

last book of the Bible, the Apocalypse or Revelation of John. The Apocalypse of John explores what will happen at the end of the world, an end which John, the author of this book, considers as impending (see Rev. 1.1: 'The revelation of Jesus Christ, which God gave him to show to his servants what must happen soon'). In our language, the words apocalyptic and apocalypse have a double meaning. On the one hand, they can refer to the Book of Revelation, so that we can speak, for instance, of 'apocalyptic riders', meaning the four riders of Revelation 6.1–8, who symbolize various disasters at the end of history. On the other hand, the words can indicate the subject-matter of the Book of Revelation. Apocalypse then means 'the end of the world' (as described in the Book of Revelation) and apocalyptic means 'concerning the end of the world'. In a somewhat wider usage, the words can also refer to what resembles the end of the world as described in the Book of Revelation, so that apocalypse receives the meaning of 'a time of chaos', 'a catastrophe', and apocalyptic the meaning of 'ominous', 'catastrophic'. So we speak of the apocalyptic view of the future of a doom-monger, and we say that a work of art such as Pablo Picasso's *Guernica* depicts apocalyptic horror.

It will be clear that when we call 2 Thessalonians an apocalyptic text, we intend to say that the letter, or at least an important part of it, deals with the end of history, of the world, and that it does so in a way which is reminiscent of the Book of Revelation. It is also obvious that when the letter is apocalyptic in this sense, it is also eschatological, that is, it concerns eschatology, the doctrine of the last things. 'Eschatological' is a very wide category, as there are many ways to speak of the 'last things'; apocalyptic indicates one special variety of eschatology (i.e. the kind of eschatology found in the Book of Revelation).

The apocalyptic eschatology of the Book of Revelation represents a certain early Jewish and early Christian way of thinking about the end of the world. It can be characterized very briefly in the following way: there are two 'ages', the present one which is bad and in which God's people are oppressed by their enemies, and the coming one which will be good and in which God's people will be saved; the present age is coming to its end and very soon God will intervene in history to bring about the new age. Such a view of the end is found not only in the Book of Revelation, but also in several other early Jewish and early Christian writings. Still within the Old Testament, we find it in such texts as Isaiah 24–7,

Joel, Zechariah 9–14 and especially in Daniel. It is well represented in the so-called Old Testament Pseudepigrapha; we could mention *1 Enoch, 4 Ezra, 2 Baruch*, the *Apocalypse of Abraham*, the *Sibylline Oracles*, the *Testament of Moses* as books which are at least partially devoted to apocalyptic eschatology. It is found in the writings of the Qumran community, especially in the *War Rule*, which is about the final, eschatological battle between the 'sons of light' and the 'sons of darkness'. In early Christian literature, we find it not only in the Book of Revelation, but also in other writings; for instance, Mark 13 (and its parallels in Matthew and Luke) and the sixteenth chapter of the *Didache* ('Teaching of the Apostles'). As said above, 2 Thessalonians is also supposed to contain apocalyptic eschatology.

Closer consideration of the writings in which apocalyptic eschatology is found reveals that within the overall scheme drawn above, many variations are possible. The interest of the writer can be focused on the fate of the people or on the fate of the individual, on a coming age on earth or in heaven; the coming age can be depicted in material or in spiritual terms, as a renewal of the present age or as the creation of something entirely different, and between all these extremes, various intermediate positions are possible.

'APOCALYPSE' AND 'APOCALYPTICISM'

Now we should be aware that the word 'apocalyptic' has been used above in the sense it has in our ordinary language. The word comes, as we saw, from a Greek verb with the meaning 'to reveal'. The kind of eschatology which I just labelled apocalyptic, occurs in fact quite often, although not exclusively, in writings which present themselves as narratives about revelations, apocalypses in the literal, Greek sense of the word; the writers of these apocalypses usually pretend to be great men from Israel's past such as Enoch, who 'walked with God, and he was not, for God took him' (Gen. 5.24), Abraham, Moses, Baruch, and Ezra (see Rowland 1982; Collins 1984). Apocalyptic eschatology has its organic place in writings which purport to render direct revelation from God, obtained in journeys through, or visions of, the heavenly world, or in dreams, or through an intermediary such as an angel. A few examples may illustrate this. In Daniel 7, Daniel sees in his dream four beasts coming out of the sea (7.1–8), the appearance of 'the ancient of days' (God himself; 7.9–10), the destruction of the fourth beast and the taking away of dominion from the three others (7.11–12), and the coming of 'one like a son of man', to whom the ancient of days gives everlasting royal power (7.13–14). He then asks 'one of those who were standing' (an angel) for an explanation of his vision, and it is given to him: the four beasts are four kingdoms, and finally the kingdom will be given to 'the saints of the Most High' (7.15–28). Here we have, first, mysterious revelation in Daniel's dream, and then its explanation by the *angelus interpres*, the 'interpreting angel'. The same pattern is found in Daniel 8, while in Daniel 9 the mysterious revelation consists in words of the prophet Jeremiah (Jer. 25.11–12; 29.10), which the angel explains; in Daniel 10–12 the revelation is entirely given in words of the angel. As we saw above, the Book of Revelation is explicitly presented as 'revelation of Jesus Christ' (1.1); it starts with John's vision of the heavenly Jesus who is 'like a son of man' (1.13), who tells him what to write in the seven letters to the seven churches of Asia (1.12–3.22). This is followed by a vision of the heavenly world with God's throne and the Lamb (chs 4–5), and there the things that are to come are revealed to the seer, when, among other things, the seven seals of the scroll in God's hand are broken by the Lamb (6.1–8.1), the seven trumpets are blown by seven angels (8.2–11.19), and the seven bowls of God's wrath are poured out by seven angels (15.1–16.21). At the end of the book we find the well-known vision of the new heaven and the new earth, and of the new Jerusalem (21.1–22.5).

Eschatology is not the only topic of the apocalypses. First of all, the view of the 'last things' is frequently coupled in the apocalypses with a view of the preceding history. In Daniel 7, for instance, the four beasts represent history up to the time of writing of the apocalypse, which is the time of the persecution of the Jews under the Syrian King Antiochus Epiphanes (175–164 BCE) and his desecration of the temple in Jerusalem (168 BCE); the destruction of the fourth beast and the giving of the kingdom to the saints of the Most High are still expected to happen in the very near future. In the so-called 'Animal Apocalypse' in *1 Enoch* (chs 85–91; this part of *1 Enoch* has to be dated to approximately the same time as Daniel), we find an extensive description of the history of Israel from Adam to the time of the Messiah, in which the acting persons are represented as various kinds of animals. Actual history can be recognized without too many problems up to 90.14, where Judas

Maccabee's defeat of the Syrian army at Bet-Zur (165 BCE) is probably told. What follows cannot be connected with what really happened, and contains the writer's view of the near future: God's judgment and his bringing about of a new Jerusalem, and the birth of the Messiah. This coupling of preceding history and expectation of what is going to happen makes it possible to date these apocalypses: what clearly constitutes a *vaticinium ex eventu* (i.e. a prediction on the basis of events; 'prediction', of course, from the perspective of the hero from the past who claims to have written the apocalypse), precedes the time of writing, the rest is the (real) writer's view of the future.

Secondly, in addition to a view of past and future history the apocalypses contain revelations about the heavenly world: about the various heavens, about the angels, about God sitting on his throne, about the movements of the sun, the moon, and the stars, about the place where the fallen angels (the 'sons of God' of Gen. 6.1–4) are, about Paradise and Gehenna (the hell). Here follows, by way of illustration, the beginning of the so-called 'Astronomical Book' (*1 Enoch* 72–82, dating from the second century BCE; bracketed words have been added by the translator):

> The Book of the Itinerary of the Luminaries of Heaven: the position of each and every one, in respect to their ranks, in respect to their authorities, and in respect to their seasons; each one according to their names and their places of origin and according to their months, which Uriel, the holy angel who was with me, and who (also) is their guide, showed me – just as he showed me all their treatises and the nature of the years of the world unto eternity, till the new creation which abides forever is created.
>
> (*1 Enoch* 72.1; trans. E. Isaac, in Charlesworth 1983: 50)

In this passage, the cosmological revelation is explicitly coupled with the eschatological revelation: the things that the angel Uriel shows to Enoch about the heavenly lights remain valid until 'the new creation which abides forever is created'. In the 'Astronomical Book' as well as in other apocalyptic writings, both eschatological and cosmological secrets are revealed to the seer.

On the basis of the above, the following definition of apocalypse will be understood:

> A genre of revelatory literature with a narrative framework, in which a revelation is mediated by an otherworldly being to a

human recipient, disclosing a transcendent reality which is both temporal, insofar as it envisages eschatological salvation, and spatial insofar as it involves another, supernatural world.

(Collins 1984: 4)

The term 'apocalypticism' should be used for 'the ideology of a movement that shares the conceptual structure of the apocalypses' (Collins 1984: 10). The term is often restricted to historically oriented apocalypticism, that is, to the kind of apocalypticism that is interested in eschatology, but when we try to keep our linguistic usage as clear as possible, we should also subsume under it the kind of apocalypticism that is interested in the heavenly world. Apocalypticism was not the ideology of one specific movement; it was shared by various movements, one of which was early Christianity.

APOCALYPTIC ESCHATOLOGY

Now we should have a closer look at the kind of eschatology found in the apocalypses, in view of the eschatological statements found in 2 Thessalonians. The simplest and clearest way to do so is to take one specific passage as the point of departure. I have chosen *1 Enoch* 1, the opening vision of the so-called 'Book of the Watchers' (*1 Enoch* 1–36, dating from before the time of the Maccabean uprising; 'Watchers' are fallen angels), because it is an early and representative specimen of apocalyptic eschatology, suitable to illustrate its characteristic traits. The chapter is also of interest because its end (1.9) is quoted in the New Testament, in Jude 14–15.

[1] The blessing of Enoch: with which he blessed the elect and the righteous who would be present on the day of tribulation at (the time of) the removal of all the ungodly ones. [2] And Enoch, the blessed and righteous man of the Lord, took up (his parable) while his eyes were open and he saw, and said, '(This is) a holy vision from the heavens which the angels showed me: and I heard from them everything and I understood. I look not for this generation but for the distant one that is coming. I speak about the elect ones and concerning them.' [3] And I took up with a parable (saying), 'The God of the universe, the Holy Great One, will come forth from his dwelling. [4] And from there he will march upon Mount Sinai and appear in his camp emerging from heaven with a mighty power. And everyone shall be afraid,

and Watchers shall quiver. [5] And great fear and trembling shall seize them unto the ends of the earth. [6] Mountains and high places will fall down and be frightened. And high hills shall be made low; and they shall melt like a honeycomb before the flame. [7] And earth shall be rent asunder; and all that is upon the earth shall perish. And there shall be a judgment upon all, (including) the righteous. [8] And to all the righteous he will grant peace. He will preserve the elect, and kindness shall be upon them. They shall all belong to God and they shall prosper and be blessed; and the light of God shall shine unto them. [9] Behold, he will arrive with ten million of the holy ones in order to execute judgment upon all. He will destroy the wicked ones and censure all flesh on account of everything that they have done, that which the sinners and the wicked ones committed against him.'

(trans. E. Isaac, in Charlesworth 1983: 13–14)

According to *1 Enoch* 1.2, Enoch reports a vision of the time of the end, which angels mediated to him from heaven. In apocalypticism, things are seen from God's perspective; that concerns both the consummation of history and the secrets of the cosmos. The literary genre of the apocalypse makes clear that the knowledge contained in such a writing is supposed to be no human knowledge, acquired via natural ways, but divine knowledge, revealed to someone elected by God. We are concerned here, of course, with what an apocalypse *pretends* to be; it remains the product of a human writer, but of one who claims to be a visionary. We should at least start by taking such claims seriously, allowing for the possibility that an apocalypse contains genuine mystical experience.

The divine quality of the knowledge mediated in an apocalypse gives it a comforting effect: the reader of an apocalypse is enabled to look through the appearances of a purely human perception of reality, and to see things as they are in God's view, as what they really are. In apocalyptic eschatology, this divine knowledge concerns the outcome of history. In Enoch's vision, the outcome consists in God's judgment upon all; the righteous will come through it, but the wicked will be destroyed (1.8–9). In the present time, it may look as if the wicked are winning and the righteous are losing, but finally things will be the other way round. Enoch receives his vision in view of 'the elect and the righteous' of the future ('future' from the perspective of Enoch as the alleged writer of the apocalypse), those who will be alive at the time of the end (1.1–2).

Apocalyptic eschatology is deterministic: what has happened in the past and what will happen in the future has been pre-determined by God. In our passage from *1 Enoch*, God's final coming and his judgment are presented as events that will un-doubtedly take place; they do not depend upon human decisions and human actions but solely upon God's decree. The only thing humans can do is to take care to belong at the critical moment to the righteous. They cannot influence the course of history, but they can take the right stance. The deterministic effect is re-inforced by the attribution of the apocalypse to a great figure from the past, in our case to Enoch, 'seventh from Adam' (Jude 14), who, as we saw, did not die a natural death but was taken away by God (Gen. 5.24), which makes him an eminently suitable recipient of revelations. The attribution to Enoch suggests that already, a very long time ago, God revealed the unchangeable course of history (cf. *1 Enoch* 1.2: 'I look not for this generation but for the distant one that is coming'). When such a revelation also com-prises a detailed description of the course of history up to the time the apocalypse was in reality written (cf. the examples of Daniel 7 and of *1 Enoch* 85–91, given above), the idea that history only follows a course determined by God becomes still stronger. God is the Lord of history.

After the above, it will be understood that apocalyptic escha-tology usually flourishes in times of crisis. We can be fairly certain that the Book of Daniel and parts of *1 Enoch* were written in the time of the persecution of the Jews under the Syrian King Antiochus Epiphanes, when the attempt was made to Hellenize the Jewish religion and way of life, and pious Jews were op-pressed. *4 Ezra*, *2 Baruch* and the *Apocalypse of Abraham* were written shortly after the fall of Jerusalem in 70 CE. The Book of Revelation was probably written towards the end of the reign of the Emperor Domitian (81–96 CE), when Christians were per-secuted in Asia Minor. All these apocalypses are products of the oppressed, and the heavenly revelations about the final outcome of history are meant to encourage them. They can be sure of the final victory, although the present reality looks quite different. It will now be clear why it has been proposed to expand the definition of apocalypse quoted above with the following words:

'intended to interpret present, earthly circumstances in light of
the supernatural world and of the future, and to influence both
the understanding and the behavior of the audience by means of
divine authority' (Yarbro Collins 1986: 7).

Apocalyptic eschatology may be considered as a form of
theodicy. The term 'theodicy', used for the first time at the end
of the seventeenth century by the German philosopher G. W.
Leibniz, derives from the Greek words *theos*, 'God', and *dikē*,
'lawsuit' or 'judgment', and means 'justification of God'. The
central question of theodicy is: how can the existence of an
almighty, good and just God be reconciled with the presence of
evil and injustice in this world?

In ancient Israelite religion, it was supposed, in a simple,
straightforward way, that God rewards obedience to his law, to
the Torah, with a long and good life (see, e.g., Lev. 18.5; Deut.
30.15–20). This view is put forward eloquently in Psalm 1, where
the way of life of the righteous, whose 'delight is in the law of the
Lord' and who 'meditates on his law day and night' (1.2), is
opposed to the way of life of the wicked. The righteous are
compared to a prospering tree planted by water (1.3), the wicked
to chaff scattered by the wind (1.4). 'The Lord knows the way
of the righteous, but the way of the wicked will perish' (1.6).
However, reality often differs from this picture. Very often the
righteous, who live in agreement with the Torah, come out worst,
and the wicked, who do not obey God, come out best. This
happens especially in situations in which the wicked persecute
the righteous, and the righteous die by the hands of the wicked.
Such a state of affairs runs counter to the ideal picture of Psalm 1
and comparable texts. The problems evoked by this state of
affairs, already known from the Old Testament Book of Job, are
expressed in *4 Ezra* 3.30–3, where Ezra is presented as saying to
God, on account of the destruction of Jerusalem by the Babylonians in 586 BCE:

And my heart failed me, for I have seen how you endure those
who sin, and have spared those who act wickedly, and have
destroyed your people, and have preserved your enemies, and
have not shown to anyone how your way may be compre-
hended. Are the deeds of Babylon better than those of Zion? Or
has another nation known you besides Israel? Or what tribes
have so believed your covenants as these tribes of Jacob? Yet their

reward has not appeared and their labor has borne no fruit. For I have traveled widely among the nations and have seen that they abound in wealth, though they are unmindful of your commandments.

(trans. B. M. Metzger, in Charlesworth 1983: 529)

Ezra receives, like Job (Job 38–41), the answer from the angel that God's ways are inscrutable (4.1–21); when Ezra repeats his questions (4.22–5), the angel replies that 'the age is hastening swiftly to its end. For it will not be able to bring the things that have been promised to the righteous in their appointed times, because this age is full of sadness and infirmities' (4.26–7; trans. B. M. Metzger, in Charlesworth 1983: 530).

If, in such situations, one does not want to abandon the idea of an almighty, good and just God, who rewards the righteous and punishes the wicked, one has to assume, to vindicate God, some kind of compensation outside this world. One has to suppose that God now allows the wicked to oppress the righteous, but that in the final outcome he will punish them. If God really is just, it is unthinkable that the present age is the only one there is; there has to be a coming age as well, in which God will adjust what he has allowed to go wrong. If God really is faithful to the covenant he made with Israel, he will not abandon those from Israel who are devoted to him. In apocalyptic eschatology, God's omnipotence, his goodness and justice are vindicated by the idea of the final judgment and of the coming age. In *1 Enoch* 1.7–9, it is said that 'there will be a judgment upon all'; God will then give peace to the righteous, who will prosper and be blessed, and he will destroy the wicked. That sounds like an eschatological transposition of the theology of Psalm 1: the reward and punishment assigned there in this life to righteous and wicked are transposed in *1 Enoch* to the coming age.

To understand apocalyptic eschatology, it is vital to see that it is a form of theodicy. In the apocalyptic view, it is not necessary to deny, under the pressure of present evil, that God governs history; God's power seems to be hidden now but it will become visible in the near future. Such a view is a source of perseverance and strength to endure under oppression and persecution. It may be a source both of passively waiting for God to intervene and of actively fighting with God against the forces of evil. An example of the former attitude may be found in the Levite Taxo mentioned in *Testament of Moses* 9; at the time of the final tribulation, he says to his sons:

> We shall fast for a three-day period and on the fourth day we shall go into a cave, which is in the open country. There let us die rather than transgress the commandments of the Lord of Lords, the God of our fathers. For if we do this, and do die, our blood will be avenged before the Lord.
>
> (9.6–7; trans. J. Priest, in Charlesworth 1983: 931)

The attitude of active fighting can be exemplified by the Qumran *War Rule*, in which the final battle is supposed to be fought by the host of heaven together with the members of the Qumran sect against the host of Belial (i.e. Satan) together with his earthly adherents. God is addressed in the following way (the square brackets indicate lacunae in the manuscript):

> Thou wilt muster the [hosts of] Thine [el]ect, in their Thousands and Myriads, with Thy Holy Ones [and with all] Thine Angels, that they may be mighty in battle, [and may smite] the rebels of the earth by Thy great judgements, and that [they may triumph] together with the elect of heaven.
>
> (12.4–5; trans. G. Vermes 1975: 139)

Apocalyptic eschatology is in any event a view of history that gives divine comfort to the oppressed.

It will be evident from the above that apocalyptic eschatology presupposes a neat and clear distinction between the righteous and the wicked, between 'we' and 'they', and that this distinction is sometimes given almost superhuman, cosmic dimensions. To us, such a distinction with such dimensions may seem to be premature, presumptuous and primitive. We should, however, take into account the following considerations: in apocalyptic eschatology the final judgment is left to God alone; the threat of judgment is also meant to induce people to make the right choice; for pious Jews, observance of the Torah is an unequivocal criterion for righteousness; in the crisis of persecution there is usually not much doubt about who belongs to which side; and it is not hard to imagine experiences that may induce people to think that both good and evil are forces that transcend human reality. We should also bear in mind that for the apocalyptic writer, the victory of the good and just God of Israel is beyond doubt. Before passing verdict on an ideology such as apocalypticism, we should first try to understand it.

THE LANGUAGE OF APOCALYPTIC ESCHATOLOGY

Because apocalyptic eschatology focuses on a future that is not yet visible, it uses a language which is not so much descriptive as evocative. It abounds in images which may be called 'mythological', because they can be traced to Near Eastern mythologies, and also because they are human efforts to objectify what cannot be objectified – God's intervention in our human world. For the writers of apocalypses, their Holy Scripture, what Christians call the Old Testament, was an important source of images to depict God's future. The prophetic books were a particularly rich source, which is not surprising given the orientation towards the future which is prominent in these books; we have already seen that parts of these books share the outlook of apocalyptic eschatology. One only needs to consult an edition of the Greek text or a translation of the Book of Revelation where in the margin or at the bottom of the page references are given to the biblical passages that inspired the writer of this apocalypse; it soon becomes evident that the text of Revelation has been influenced very heavily by the Old Testament (see further Beale 1988).

When we turn to our sample passage *1 Enoch* 1, we can observe there the same influence of various Old Testament passages. Immediately at the beginning we find the words: 'The blessing of Enoch: with which he blessed the elect and the righteous' (1.1). This looks like a studied parallel to Deuteronomy 33.1: 'This is the blessing with which Moses, the man of God, blessed the children of Israel before his death'. Note also that in *1 Enoch* 1.2, Enoch is characterized as 'the blessed and righteous man of the Lord', and that 1.8–9 contains parallels to Deuteronomy 33.2 (see below, p. 56).

In *1 Enoch* 1.2, it is said of Enoch that he 'took up (his parable)', and this is repeated in 1.3 in the first person: 'I took up with a parable'. It is further said of him that 'his eyes were open and he saw', and the object of his vision is 'a holy vision from the heavens which the angels showed me; and I heard from them everything and I understood' (1.2). This picture of Enoch derives from the picture of Balaam in Numbers 23–4. When the people of Israel, on their way to the promised land, are camping in the plains of Moab, and Moab takes fright at them, King Balak of Moab requests the prophet Balaam to curse Israel. Balaam, who speaks of what God reveals to him (cf. 23.3), instead blesses Israel. All oracles delivered by Balaam are introduced by words that can be translated: 'And he took up his parable' (23.7, 18; 24.3, 15, 20, 21, 23). The third and fourth oracles begin with almost identical words: 'Oracle of Balaam, the son of Beor, oracle of the man whose eye is opened, oracle of the one who hears the words of God (...), who sees the vision of the Almighty, who falls with eyes uncovered' (24.3–4, 15–16). There is a striking agreement between Balaam and Enoch; an interesting difference is that Balaam receives his vision immediately from God, and Enoch through the angels. In apocalypticism, there is a great distance between God and the earth, and a host of angels mediates between God and humanity.

The idea that God 'will come forth from his dwelling' (*1 Enoch* 1.3) for judgment is also found in Isaiah 26.21 and Micah 1.3. The latter Old Testament passage in particular seems to have inspired the writer of *1 Enoch* 1. It continues: 'And he [God] will tread upon the heights of the earth'; *1 Enoch* 1.4 speaks more specifically of God who 'will march upon Mount Sinai', the 'classical' place of revelation (see, e.g., Exodus 19). In *1 Enoch* 1.6–7, it continues: 'Mountains and high places...shall melt like a honeycomb before the flame. And earth shall be rent asunder'. With these words, one should compare Micah 1.4: 'And mountains shall melt under him, and the valleys shall be cleft, like wax before the fire'.

At the end of *1 Enoch* 1, the words 'Behold, he will arrive with ten million of the holy ones' (1.9) have been influenced by Deuteronomy 33.2, where God's coming 'from Sinai' is said to be, at least in a possible reconstruction of the text, 'with ten thousands of holy ones'. In *1 Enoch*, the reference to God's coming is preceded by 'And the light of God shall shine unto them' (1.8). These words are reminiscent of other elements in the theophany of Deuteronomy 33.2: 'The Lord came from Sinai, and dawned unto them from Seir, he shone forth from Mount Paran' (cf. also, e.g., Is. 9.1).

It will be clear from the above that in the opening chapter of *1 Enoch*, various passages from Scripture have been influential. In many instances, it is impossible to relate the words of the apocalyptic writer to one specific Old Testament passage, while it is at the same time obvious that they have been influenced by scriptural ideas and images. So the idea that the mountains will be frightened when God comes (*1 Enoch* 1.6) is found several times in the Old Testament (see, e.g., Nah. 1.5; Hab. 3.6; Psalm 114). The language of the apocalyptic writers has evidently been drenched in the language of the Old Testament; they make a creative use of their religious heritage to address in their own time the problem of

God's seeming absence. We shall see in the commentary below that the writer of 2 Thessalonians with his apocalyptic eschatology is no exception to this rule.

APOCALYPTIC ESCHATOLOGY IN EARLY CHRISTIANITY

In many respects early Christianity can be characterized as an apocalyptic movement. To begin with, apocalypses – direct revelations in dreams or visions or through an angel – have an important place in it as a means of communication between God and man (see Rowland 1982: 358–441). It is told in Mark's Gospel that when Jesus was baptized by John, 'he saw the heavens tear apart and the Spirit descend upon him like a dove' (1.10). Jesus' transfiguration (Mark 9.2–8 and parallels) is told as a vision granted to the disciples. According to Luke 10.18, Jesus says to his disciples: 'I saw Satan fall like lightning from heaven'. Just before Stephen is stoned, he looks intently into heaven, and he sees God's glory and Jesus standing at the right hand of God (Acts 7.55). According to Acts 10.9–16, Peter has a vision in which God reveals to him that all animals are clean and can be eaten. Paul calls his meeting with the risen Christ on the road to Damascus (Acts 9.1–9; 22.6–11; 26.12–18) a 'heavenly vision' (Acts 26.19), and in Galatians 1.15–16 he describes this experience as a revelation, by God, of God's Son. In 2 Corinthians 12.2–4, Paul writes about 'a man in Christ' (by whom he means himself), who was 'caught up to the third heaven', and 'caught up into Paradise', where he 'heard things not to be said, which a human being is not allowed to speak'. The Book of Revelation has already been discussed above in its quality of apocalypse. Outside the New Testament, a series of visions is described in, among other writings, the so-called *Shepherd of Hermas* (dating from *c.* 150 CE).

More important for our present purposes is that the nucleus of Jesus' message (in so far we can reconstruct it in a critical way), his proclamation of the kingdom of God, displays aspects that make it akin to apocalyptic eschatology. The kingdom of God 'has drawn near' (Mark 1.15; Matt. 4.17), and it will soon 'come with power' (Mark 9.1); it is equivalent to 'life' or 'eternal life' (see Mark 9.43–7; 10.17, 24–5), which is found 'in the coming age' (Mark 10.30; Luke 18.30), and it is pictured as a festive banquet (Matt. 8.11; Luke 13.28–9; cf. *1 Enoch* 62.14). The kingdom of God can also be said to be present already in Jesus' person and in his activity: the struggle against the demonic powers (Matt 12.28; Luke 11.20; 17.20–1). These very few and summary indications may show that, in Jesus' proclamation, the kingdom of God is the salvation, both to be realized soon in the coming age, and already present in Jesus' ministry. Important aspects of Jesus' proclamation of the kingdom of God have to be understood within the framework of apocalyptic eschatology.

Very soon after Jesus' death, his disciples began to believe and to proclaim that God had raised Jesus from among the dead, and that Jesus was now in heaven as Christ and Lord (see, e.g., Acts 2.24, 32–3, 36; Rom. 10.9; 1 Thess. 4.14). Resurrection of the dead had become one of the current elements of apocalyptic eschatology (see, e.g., Dan. 12.2; *1 Enoch* 91.10; 92.3), and it is easy to understand that Jesus' resurrection was also conceived as an anticipation of the final resurrection, as Paul explains in detail in 1 Corinthians 15. The resurrection of Jesus, who in his earthly ministry had inaugurated the kingdom of God, was considered as the beginning of the final resurrection of the dead. It is only logical that when apocalyptic eschatology is further developed in circles of Christians of Jewish origin, the raised and living Jesus is assigned an essential role in the events of the end. He will come from heaven and fulfil his eschatological task. So Paul writes in 1 Thessalonians that the Thessalonians were converted to God 'to await his Son from heaven, Jesus who saves us from the coming wrath' (1.10). Elsewhere in the same letter, in a passage already referred to above, Paul speaks of 'the coming (*parousia*) of the Lord', which he expects to happen in his own lifetime, and at which 'the Lord will come down from heaven', and those who belong to him, dead and living, will be with him (4.15–17). In these texts, Jesus is supposed to return from heaven, where he has been since his resurrection, and to save those who belong to him. His role as judge of the living and the dead becomes a standard element of his eschatological function (see, e.g., Acts 17.31; 2 Cor. 5.10; 2 Tim. 4.1). Originally God was thought to be the eschatological judge (see, e.g., Is. 3.13–14; Rom. 3.6), but this function was transferred to Jesus; in a comparable way, 'that son of man', who is also called the Righteous One, the Elect One or the Messiah, executes judgment in *1 Enoch* 37–71. It is not astonishing that Jesus is identified with the heavenly 'son of man' from Daniel 7.13–14, to whom God gives dominion, glory and kingdom, and that Jesus' eschatological role is pictured in terms of the apocalyptic 'son of man' (see, e.g., Mark 13.26–7 and parallels; Mark 14.62 and parallels; Matt. 25.31–46; Rev. 1.7, 13–16). The difficult and intriguing question – whether the historical Jesus considered himself, explicitly or implicitly, as the Danielic son of man or as the Messiah or as another eschatological agent – can be left aside here (see about such problems De Jonge 1991); for our purposes, it is sufficient to observe that soon after Jesus' death, Christians, believing that God had raised him from among the dead, began to assign such qualities to him, and expected him to function as God's eschatological agent at the impending end of this age. These Christians considered themselves as living in two ages at the same time: by their faith in Jesus, they already participated in the coming age, inaugurated by his ministry and his resurrection, but the present age with all its negative aspects was still the reality of their daily life (cf., e.g., Rom. 12.2; Gal. 1.4).

It will be clear from the above, that apocalyptic eschatology constitutes an important part of the conceptual framework not only of Jesus' proclamation of the kingdom of God, but also of the early Christian proclamation of Jesus. More than once we find Paul using the language of apocalyptic eschatology. I have already had the opportunity to refer to 1 Thessalonians 4.15–17. Another Pauline passage where we meet explicit apocalyptic eschatology is 1 Corinthians 15. Here, Paul clearly uses the language of apocalyptic eschatology when he speaks of Christ's subjugation of all negative powers and his final submission to God (15.23–8), and of the transformation of the living at the parousia (15.51–5).

As said above, there are some early Christian texts in which apocalyptic eschatology is the explicit theme. Within the New Testament, apocalyptic eschatology is most evidently found, apart from the Book of Revelation, in Mark 13 and parallels, a passage often called the 'synoptic apocalypse'. In Mark 13 (for the sake of simplicity, I leave aside the parallels in Matthew and Luke), Jesus predicts the destruction of the temple (13.2), whereupon his disciples ask him when these things will happen, and what sign there will be that they will all be accomplished (13.3–4). Jesus then announces what is to come: false Messiahs and false prophets will appear and they will lead may people astray, wars will be fought, there will be earthquakes and famines, the disciples will be persecuted (13.5–23), in short: 'Those days will constitute an oppression such as there has not been from the beginning of the creation which God created until now, and will not be' (13.19). After that, strange physical phenomena will occur (13.24–5), 'and then they will see the son of man come in clouds with great power and glory' (13.26), to gather his elect (13.27). Jesus is presented as telling all this with a clear 'pastoral' aim: to prevent the disciples' being led astray or alarmed (13.5, 7), to exhort them to be on their guard and to keep watch (13.9, 23, 33–7). Jesus is, in Mark's view (cf. 1.10–11), the one who knows, the one who is able, in apocalyptic fashion, to see history from God's perspective (which does not mean that he knows everything, see 13.32); therefore he can tell his disciples what will happen and reassure them. Jesus fulfils the role which the hero from Israel's past fulfils in Jewish apocalypses: on the basis of his supernatural knowledge, he announces the events of the end. We probably have here a *vaticinium ex eventu*, just as we observed it to be the case in other apocalypses: we can perceive, in the text of the apocalypse, the actual course of history until the time the book was written. Mark 13.5–23 seems to reflect the circumstances during the Jewish War of 66–70 CE, or at least the circumstances at the eve of the war. (As there is in Mark no unambiguous reference to the fall of Jerusalem, in contrast to Luke 19.43–4; 21.20–4, we have to date the Gospel of Mark to shortly before the fall of the city.) Anyhow, the partial fulfilment of what Jesus has announced to his disciples serves to reinforce the expectation of the reader or hearer that everything will take place as Jesus has said. It is not astonishing that precisely on the point of transition from what has happened (at the moment Mark writes his gospel) to what still has to happen, Jesus says to the disciples: 'Be on your guard; I have told you all things beforehand' (13.23).

Another early Christian text marked by apocalyptic eschatology is the final chapter of the *Didache* (this writing dates from the beginning of the second century CE); here follows an English translation of *Didache* 16:

[1] Keep watch over your life; let your lamps not go out, and let your loins not weaken, but be ready; for you do not know the hour when our Lord will come. [2] You should come together often, searching for what is useful for your souls; for the entire time of your faith will be of no avail to you, if you will not become perfect in the time of the end. [3] For in the last days false prophets and corrupters will become numerous, and sheep will turn into wolves, and love will turn into hatred; [4] for when

lawlessness increases, they will hate and persecute and betray each other, and then the deceiver of the world will appear like the son of God and perform signs and wonders, and the earth will be delivered into his hands, and he will do outrages such as have never happened from eternity. [5] Then mankind will come into the fire of trial, and many will stumble and perish, but those who remain steadfast in their faith will be saved by the cursed one himself [i.e. Jesus, cf. Gal. 3.13]. [6] And then the signs of truth will appear: first the sign that heaven opens, then the sign of the sound of the trumpet, and thirdly the rising of the dead; [7] not of all, but as it was said: The Lord will come and all saints with him [Zech. 14.5]. [8] Then the world will see the Lord come on the clouds of heaven to repay everyone according to his acts.

We meet in this text several traits which are by now more or less familiar: the hortatory function of the apocalyptic eschatology (16.1–2), the crisis preceding the end (16.3–5), Jesus as the saviour who comes from heaven (16.6–8), the resurrection of the dead (16.6). A trait which we have not yet met is that the increasing evil just before the end is personified into one human figure, called here 'the deceiver of the world', who behaves like Christ, performing signs and wonders (16.4). Such a concentration of eschatological evil into one human being is also found elsewhere. In *2 Baruch* 40.1–2, for instance, God says to Baruch about the end (in the course of the explanation of a dream):

The last ruler who is left alive at that time will be bound, whereas the entire host will be destroyed. And they will carry him on Mount Zion, and my Anointed One will convict him of all his wicked deeds and will assemble and set before him all the works of his hosts. And after these things he will kill him and protect the rest of my people who will be found in the place that I have chosen.

(trans. A. F. J. Klijn, in Charlesworth 1983: 633)

In Revelation 13.1–18, 16.13–14, 19.20, and 20.10, we encounter the figures of the beast, who evidently represents a human being (the Roman Emperor), and of the false prophet who propagates the cult of the beast; the power of the beast derives from the dragon, depicted in Revelation 12, who is Satan (12.9). In Christian circles, the eschatological antagonist-imitator of Christ is sometimes called 'the antichrist' (see, e.g., 1 John 2.18); he will perform, in a Christ-like manner, signs and wonders (amply listed in the third chapter of the *Apocalypse of Elijah*, a Christian writing probably dating from the third century CE), and he will finally be defeated by God's eschatological agent (see further Jenks 1991).

APOCALYPTIC ESCHATOLOGY IN 2 THESSALONIANS

The eschatological antagonist of Christ brings us back to 2 Thessalonians, for in the second chapter of the letter this figure plays an essential role. When we read 2 Thessalonians in the light of the above, it will become clear that its distinctive ideas indeed belong in the realm of apocalyptic eschatology.

The author of the letter explicitly states that his addressees find themselves in a situation of crisis: they are persecuted and oppressed (1.4). That is considered as a token of God's just judgment: God will repay their oppressors with oppression, and the addressees will enjoy liberation in God's kingdom, when the Lord Jesus will be revealed from heaven to punish the wicked and to be glorified in his faithful (1.5–10). This entire picture looks very much like a Christianized version of the scheme we found in our sample text *1 Enoch* 1.7–9: at the end, God will judge all mankind, he will give peace to the righteous and destroy the wicked. The differences are that in 2 Thessalonians, both God and Jesus are supposed to act as judges, and that the author of 2 Thessalonians is apparently less interested in the physical phenomena of the end than the writer of *1 Enoch* 1 (see 1.6–7).

In 2 Thessalonians 2, the addressees are requested not to be alarmed by the false message that the day of the Lord has come (2.1–2). That day has not yet come, because other events have to occur first: the apostasy and the revelation of the man of lawlessness; the addressees know about these things (2.3–5). The appearance of the lawless one is still thwarted by a restraining power or person (2.6–7); after the lawless one has appeared, with his demonic power and false signs and wonders and his deceit, by which he deludes unbelievers, he will be destroyed by the Lord Jesus (2.8–12). The false idea that the day of the Lord has come, finds a parallel in Jesus' warning that many will come in his name, passing themselves off as Christ returned on earth (Mark 13.6, 21–2 and parallels); the most reasonable explanation for this warning is, as we shall see in the commentary below (see pp. 100–1), that there were indeed people who claimed to be or were supposed to be Christ returned on earth, at least at the time Mark's Gospel was composed. We have already met the apostasy (in many forms) preceding the day of the Lord, in Mark 13 and parallels, in *Didache* 16, and in Revelation, but the idea is by no means restricted to Christian apocalyptic eschatology, as is evident from, for example, *4 Ezra* 5.1–2, where the angel Uriel says to Ezra:

> Behold, the days are coming when those who dwell on earth shall be seized with great terror, and the way of truth shall be hidden, and the land shall be barren of faith. And unrighteousness shall be increased beyond what you yourself see, and beyond what you heard of formerly.
>
> (trans. B. M. Metzger, in Charlesworth 1983: 531–2)

For parallels to the coming and annihilation of the eschatological antagonist of Christ, I refer to the end of the preceding section. It is not so easy to adduce parallels for the restraining power or person mentioned in 2 Thessalonians 2.6–7; however, it will appear below in the commentary that this figure can also be situated within apocalyptic eschatology.

In the third chapter of 2 Thessalonians, apocalyptic eschatology is largely missing. The specific problem dealt with in that chapter is that some members of the church behave 'in a disorderly way and not in accord with the tradition' (3.6), and refuse to work for a living, taking instead advantage of others and busying themselves with useless things, causing unrest (3.6–12). It will be shown in our commentary that this disorderly conduct is a direct consequence of the eschatological error combated in chapter 2. To put it briefly: when the day of the Lord has arrived, there is no need to work any longer. So there is a clear link between chapter 3 and the apocalyptic eschatology of chapter 2.

2 Thessalonians is apparently to be situated in Christian circles with a good deal of interest in apocalyptic eschatology. Both 2 Thessalonians and the 'synoptic apocalypse' show that here and there in such circles it was declared that the day of the Lord had arrived, that Christ had returned. The usual reaction to this declaration is to point to what still has to happen before the parousia, but this reaction remains within the same framework of apocalyptic eschatology.

Although 2 Thessalonians is marked by apocalyptic eschatology, it is not an apocalypse in the strict sense: 'Paul' does not report revelations he has received about the end of history. One could be tempted to compare the attribution of the letter to Paul with the attribution of apocalypses to great figures from the past or with the attribution of the 'synoptic apocalypse' to Jesus (so Holland 1990), but in that case the letter would constitute an apocalypse only in a very remote sense, because the essential aspect of revelation to the figure of the past, in this case Paul, is missing. Besides, the attribution of letters to Paul has occurred elsewhere in early Christianity without any perceptible apocalyptic relevance. As remarked above, apocalyptic eschatology is also found outside apocalypses in the strict sense, although it carries with it something of its organic setting within an apocalypse, namely that history is seen from God's perspective and God's intention.

PLACE AND DATE OF COMPOSITION OF 2 THESSALONIANS

The final question to be asked in this chapter is whether our findings concerning the religious milieu of 2 Thessalonians, together with some of our earlier results, give us some clues about the place and date of composition of the letter. The Christian interest in explicit apocalyptic eschatology and its derailment into a realized eschatology (the idea that the day of the Lord has already arrived) may have originated in the land of Israel. The apocalyptic eschatology and the warning against realized eschatology that we find in Matthew 24.26–7, 37–41 and Luke 17.23–4, 26–35 (without a parallel in Mark), must have been already in the common source of Matthew and Luke usually called 'Q' (an abbreviation of the German *Quelle*), and this source was probably compiled in the land of Israel. Apocalyptic eschatology and its distortion into realized eschatology were then presumably intensified by the events of the Jewish War of 66–70 CE, and worked through later in several other areas. Asia Minor was one of these: it was the cradle of the Book of Revelation (see Rev. 1.4, 9–11), and also, halfway through the second century CE, of Montanism (a movement founded in Phrygia by a certain Montanus, who preached that the end of the world was near).

It is further clear from 2 Thessalonians itself that both the author and the addressees of the letter are suffering persecution (1.4; 3.2). How intense or widespread this persecution was, or who the persecutors were, does not become clear from the text. Asia Minor anyhow meets the condition of an area where persecution took place: we know that Christians were persecuted there towards the end of the reign of Domitian (81–96 CE). However, small-scale persecutions may have occurred at various times and at various places (see, e.g., 1 Thess. 2.14–16).

Another condition which the surmised place of origin of 2 Thessalonians must meet, is that Paul and his letters, at least 1 Thessalonians, have been influential there. Asia Minor fulfils that condition: it was, with Greece, Paul's major missionary area. That the letter has been addressed to the church of Thessalonica, is, as I said above, a literary expedient, connected with the use of 1 Thessalonians as a model. So we can conclude, by way of an educated guess, that Asia Minor has at least a reasonable chance to be the region where 2 Thessalonians was written.

When we try to determine the time of writing of the letter as closely as possible, we can say at least that it was written some time after Paul; that letters were written by others in Paul's name while Paul was still alive, is not very probable. A certain time has also to have elapsed for 1 Thessalonians to become known outside Thessalonica and to acquire a certain status as 'a letter from Paul', so that the author of 2 Thessalonians could use Paul's letter as a model. It will be clear that his use of 1 Thessalonians makes it possible that he knew other Pauline letters as well.

The earliest external testimony to the existence of 2 Thessalonians is found in the middle of the second century CE in Marcion's list of Pauline letters. A letter of Polycarp, Bishop of Smyrna, to the church of Philippi, probably written c. 115 CE, contains two expressions that resemble expressions from 2 Thessalonians (the pertinent part of Polycarp's letter is known to us only in a Latin translation of the Greek original). Polycarp writes about Paul, who 'boasts about you [the Philippian church] among all congregations' (11.3), and he admonishes them concerning a certain sinner and his wife: 'Do not consider such people as enemies, but call them back as suffering and erring members' (11.4). The quoted fragments resemble 2 Thessalonians 1.4 and 3.15, but Polycarp does not indicate in any way that he derives his words from 2 Thessalonians, and the real agreements concern in both cases only a few words. It would be a bit rash, therefore, to consider Polycarp's text as evidence that he knew 2 Thessalonians. We can only conclude then, again by way of educated guesswork, that 2 Thessalonians was written some time between the year 80 and the early second century CE (the same opinion on place and date of composition in Trilling 1980: 27–8).

CONCLUSION

In this chapter, we discussed the religious milieu of 2 Thessalonians. In the view of apocalyptic eschatology, God is expected to bring about the imminent end of the present bad age and to save his elect who will participate in the coming good age. This eschatology is at home in apocalypses – writings which purport to render direct revelation from God mostly to heroes from the past. The objects of revelation are past and future history, and the heavenly world. In apocalyptic eschatology, future history is consequently viewed from the perspective of God: God has predetermined the course of history and he will finally punish the wicked and save the righteous. Such an eschatology intends to offer comfort and perspective to those who are now oppressed for the sake of righteousness. It can be considered as a form of theodicy: in the coming age, the almighty, good and just God will adjust what he has allowed to go wrong in the present age. Apocalyptic eschatology uses imaginative, often mythological, language; the Old Testament has been an important source for it.

Both Jesus' own message and the early Christian message about Jesus show traits of apocalyptic eschatology. The first Christians expected the risen Jesus to return from heaven to be God's eschatological agent: to be judge and saviour of believers. Apocalyptic eschatology is the explicit theme of such early Christian texts as the Book of Revelation, Mark 13 and parallels, and *Didache* 16. 2 Thessalonians is also largely marked by apocalyptic eschatology, most clearly in chapters 1 and 2. According to 2 Thessalonians 2, the day of the Lord is not yet present; first the eschatological antagonist of Christ has to appear and apostasy has to occur, and these events are still thwarted by a restraining power or person.

2 Thessalonians with its apocalyptic eschatology may have been written in Asia Minor, some time between the year 80 and the early second century CE.

Part 2

A commentary on
2 Thessalonians

Chapter 4

The structure of 2 Thessalonians

INTRODUCTION

We shall now discuss the structure of 2 Thessalonians, that is, the main divisions of the letter, the way each of its parts has been built, and the relationship between these parts. If we want to gain a clear understanding of the message the author of the letter communicates to his readers, we have to investigate the literary means he has used to organize his message. In such an investigation, we have to take into account the literary genre of the letter (especially that of the Pauline letter) with its own conventions, the formal literary features of the text such as antithesis or repetition of words, phrases or ideas, and the content of the letter. From the letter pattern of 2 Thessalonians, it is clear that 1.1–2 constitute the epistolary prescript, and that 3.17–18 certainly belong to the letter-closing.

2 THESSALONIANS 1.3–12

The prescript of 2 Thessalonians is – as is usual in the Pauline letters – followed by a thanksgiving (1.3–4), which is taken up, after intervening thoughts, in a prayer-report (1.11–12; cf. Phil. 1.9; Col. 1.9). The body of the letter begins with 2.1: the formula 'we beg you' is characteristic of such a beginning, the vocative 'brothers and sisters' marks the transition, and the main theme of the letter is introduced with the preposition 'concerning' (see Schnider and Stenger 1987: 43).

The unity of 1.3–12 having been provisionally established, we must now examine the structure of this passage. The initial thanksgiving in the strict sense consists of 1.3–4 (see Schubert 1939: 44–6).

The obligation to thank God is explained by the congregation's progress in faith and love; the consequence of this progress is, in turn, that 'Paul' boasts among the churches about their endurance and faith in persecutions and oppressions.

Now there is, as suggested above, a clear correspondence between 1.3–4 and 1.11–12. The agreement in wording is remarkable:

1.3   we are bound to thank God always for you
1.11   to this end we always pray for you

The congregation's progress in faith and love was the reason for the author's thanksgiving; the content of his prayer is that God may make them worthy of their calling and may bring to fulfilment every good resolution and work of faith. 'Paul' prays for the completion of that for which he gave thanks. Their progress has his boasting as its consequence; God's action in continuing this progress has as its goal the mutual glorification of the Lord Jesus and the church (1.4, 12).

In what comes between the verses just discussed, the persecutions and afflictions which the congregation is suffering are said to be a token of God's just judgment, which consists in the retribution of oppression to the oppressors and of liberation to the oppressed. 'Paul' mentions the occasion of the retribution (the revelation of the Lord Jesus), and then returns to the theme of the retribution. Again he first mentions the unbelievers, who will be punished, and then, in a subordinate temporal clause, the believers – including the congregation addressed in the letter (1.10) – in whom the Lord will be glorified and admired at his coming. So the eschatological retribution is dealt with twice in this passage: in 1.5–7a and in 1.8b–10; in between, in 1.7b–8a, we hear about the appearance of the executor of the retribution.

The above means that 2 Thessalonians 1.3–12 has been built according to a concentric pattern:

A   1.3–4   thanksgiving for the congregation's progress in
               Christian life
B   1.5–7a   the eschatological retribution
C   1.7b–8a   the revelation of the Lord Jesus
B' 1.8b–10   the eschatological retribution
A' 1.11–12   prayer-report, that God may bring the
               congregation's Christian life to fulfilment

2 THESSALONIANS 2.1–17

As said above, the main theme of the letter is introduced in 2.1–2: the addressees are warned, concerning Christ's parousia and their being gathered to him, not to be confused because of a prophetic utterance or a message or a letter purporting to come 'from us', as if the day of the Lord were present. The admonition against possible sources of deception is resumed in 2.3a, and only with 2.3b does the author begin telling what has to happen before the day of the Lord.

After an instruction about what has to occur (2.3b–12) and a second thanksgiving (2.13–14), 'Paul' concludes in 2.15 that the congregation has to stand firm and to hold fast to the traditions they have been taught by his word or letter. This exhortation obviously links up with the earlier warning, and intends to change the congregation's mental agitation into mental stability:

2.1	brothers and sisters...	2.15	brothers and sisters
2.2	do not rashly lose your senses		stand firm
	and do not be alarmed...		and hold fast...
	by a word		either by our word
	or by a letter purporting to be		or by our letter
	from us		

The eschatological teaching of 2.3b–12, which is included between warning and exhortation, displays a concentric structure. The author first mentions what has to happen before the day of the Lord: the coming of the apostasy and the revelation of 'the man of lawlessness' (2.3). The latter is also qualified as 'the son of perdition' (at the end of 2.3); the additional description of his behaviour in 2.4, his making himself a god, is an elaboration of his first title. After having recalled his earlier oral teaching on these topics (2.5), 'Paul' speaks about the mysterious figure of the restraining power or person (2.6–7); whatever its meaning and identity may be, its work precedes in time the revelation of the lawless one. To him the author returns in 2.8, in wording strongly reminiscent of 2.3:

2.8   the lawless one will be revealed
2.3   the man of lawlessness is revealed

This time his second title from 2.3, 'the son of perdition', is worked out: he will be annihilated by the Lord Jesus. The further description of his activity in 2.9–12 concerns his leading astray those who refused to believe the truth. So these verses may be considered as the elaboration of the apostasy mentioned in 2.3 ('takes place' and 'sends' in 2.9, 11 are 'futuristic presents').

On the basis of the above, we may draw up the following scheme for 2 Thessalonians 2:

A   2.1–3a   warning
B   2.3b   the apostasy, and
C   2.3b–5   the revelation of the man of lawlessness, the son of
                perdition
D   2.5–7   the restraining power/person
C' 2.8   the revelation and annihilation of the lawless one
B' 2.9–12   his leading astray the unbelievers
A' 2.15   exhortation

(It seems that 2.5 belongs to both C and D, to the former because of 'these things', to the latter because of the opposition between 'when I was still' and 'and now'.)

In this scheme, the thanksgiving of 2.13–14 is still missing. What is its function? First of all, it contrasts the future salvation of the congregation with the future destruction of the unbelievers as spoken about in 2.10–12. Secondly, it takes up the topics mentioned at the beginning of this part of the letter: 'the coming of our Lord Jesus Christ and his gathering of us to himself' (2.1). They return here: God chose them 'to find salvation' (2.13), and he called them 'so that you may obtain the glory of our Lord Jesus Christ' (2.14). Thirdly, this thanksgiving is evidently meant to recall the first thanksgiving in 1.3–12. Its beginning in 2.13 is closely similar to 1.3, and both thanksgivings share the themes of God's calling (1.11; 2.14), the gospel (1.8; 2.14), and the acquiring of glory (1.10, 12; 2.14). The general line of thought is similar in 1.3–12 and 2.13–14: 'Paul' thanks God because of the Christian life of the congregation in view of Christ's parousia.

The purpose of inserting a second thanksgiving here is to stress the importance of the preceding eschatological teaching, and especially of the consequent exhortation in 2.15: if the congregation holds fast to the teaching of 'Paul', they will participate in God's final salvation. The same purpose is served by the addition of a prayer in 2.16–17, after the exhortation. In it, the author indirectly addresses Christ and God, who 'gave eternal comfort and good hope' (2.16), which also refers, within the given framework, to the preceding eschatological instruction. The content of the prayer is that Christ and God 'may...comfort your hearts and strengthen them' (2.17); this takes up the exhortation: 'stand firm and hold fast' (2.15). And just as the thanksgiving in 2.13–14 recalled the initial thanksgiving, so the end of the prayer announces the ensuing exhortation of chapter 3 (cf. esp. 2.17 with 3.3, 5).

2 THESSALONIANS 3.1–16

It is sometimes supposed that a new part, which runs through until 3.5 or even further, starts at 2.13 (so, e.g., Jewett 1986: 80; Sumney 1990, who also unconvincingly parallels 1.3–12 with 2.13–3.5). This position seems untenable, not only because of the literary unity of chapter 2, but also because of that of 3.1–16. That this part consists of exhortation, is immediately evident. The word 'finally' at its beginning (3.1), suggests that the final part of the letter now starts; the request to pray for 'Paul' (3.1–2) is a customary part of such a final section, as is also the prayer at its end (3.16; see Schnider and Stenger 1987: 76–83, 87–91). It can be shown that this final part also displays a concentric structure.

In 3.6–12, the author deals with the members of the congregation who behave in a disorderly way. He begins and ends this passage with injunctions concerning them ('we command', 3.6, 12; already used in 3.4 to announce the theme). The first one (3.6) is directed to the other members of the community: they should hold aloof from the disorderly brothers and sisters. The second one (3.12) is destined for the disorderly ones: they should 'eat their own bread, doing work in quietness'; it is preceded in 3.11 by a clause which reintroduces the disorderly ones after the digression of 3.7–10. The literal agreements between 3.6 on the one hand and 3.11–12 on the other are obvious:

3.6 we command...in the name	3.12 we command...in
of our Lord Jesus Christ	the Lord Jesus Christ
who lives in a disorderly way	3.11 living...in a disorderly way

The sequence of the agreeing elements is inverted in 3.11–12 in comparison with 3.6.

Between the two injunctions, 'Paul' puts forth his own past behaviour towards the congregation as an example worthy of imitation: he did not behave in a disorderly way, but earned his own bread (3.7–10).

So, the unit 3.6–12 has apparently been built according to an

A-B-A'-scheme. What precedes in 3.1–5 is a series of sentences loosely connected among each other. The author asks the congregation to pray for him, that his preaching may be successful, and that he may be saved 'from wicked and evil people; for faith is not everyone's business' (3.1–2). The word 'faith' in 3.2 is followed in 3.3 by 'the Lord is faithful'. In addition to this connection by catchword, there is, between the two verses, a connection of content: the faith of the congregation, strengthened and guarded from the evil one by the Lord, stands in contrast to the unbelief of the evil people who threaten 'Paul'. His trust in the Lord who strengthens and guards the congregation makes him say in 3.4 that they are doing and will continue to do what he orders. With 3.5, the author finally gives his confidence the form of a prayer.

The concluding verses 3.13–16 are comparable with 3.1–5 in that they also constitute a series of loosely connected sentences. The series begins with a general exhortation not to tire of doing good (3.13). By way of contrast, the author gives in 3.14–15 his instruction about how to deal with a person who 'does not obey our word in this letter'. The prayer of 3.16, that the Lord of peace may give them peace, links up very well with this instruction about how to deal with conflicts within the church, and so does the added prayer: 'The Lord be with you all'. The entire verse 3.16 is a prayer for the unity of the congregation.

Now the two passages 3.1–5 and 3.13–16 correspond at several points. Over against the specific instruction about the disorderly ones in 3.6–12, the exhortations contained in 3.1–5, 13–16 are vague and hardly related to a specific problem in the congregation. Both passages have at their beginning, just as 3.6–12, the address 'brothers and sisters'. They contain imperatives (3.1, 13, 14, 15), which the central section does not. Both end with a prayer which concerns the Christian life of the community (3.5, 16). In 3.1–5, 'Paul' requests them to pray for the glorious course of the *word* of the Lord and for his deliverance from wicked and evil people, and he is confident that they *do* and will *do* what he orders. In 3.13–15, he exhorts them not to tire of *doing* good, and advises them how to deal with those inside the community who oppose his *word*.

So we arrive at the following scheme for 3.1–16:

A   3.1–5   exhortation to pray for the success of the preaching of 'Paul' in his conflict with unbelievers, his trust that the community does his orders, followed by a prayer

B   3.6   injunction to hold aloof from disorderly brothers
                and sisters
C   3.7–10   the example of 'Paul'
B' 3.11–12   injunction to the disorderly brothers and sisters
A' 3.13–16   exhortation to do good and to deal rightly with
                those who disobey the word of 'Paul', followed by
                a prayer

THE CONNECTIONS BETWEEN THE THREE PARTS

Now that we have established the main parts of 2 Thessalonians and
the way each of these has been constructed, we have to explore the
connections among them; a clear pattern in these would confirm
the division of the letter proposed above.

Each of the three parts ends with a prayer for the progress in
Christian life of the congregation: a prayer-report in 1.11–12,
adapted in form to the thanksgiving which it closes, and a prayer in
2.16–17 and 3.16, in both instances beginning with an emphatic
'may the Lord...himself'. Just as in part 1 the prayer-report (1.11–12)
corresponds to the beginning of the thanksgiving (1.3–4), so the
prayer at the end of part 3 (3.16) finds its counterpart in the prayer
at its beginning (3.5). The terms which are used to describe the
Christian life of the congregation are different, though there is a
striking similarity between the beginnings of parts 1 and 3: 'faith',
'love', and 'steadfastness' occur in 1.3–4, and in 3.5 we find 'love'
and 'steadfast expectation' (in fact, in both 1.4 and 3.5 the same
Greek word *hupomonē*, 'steadfastness', is used; see the commentary
on 3.5 below), preceded by an indirect reference to the 'faith' of
the congregation in 3.2.

At the end of part 1, 'Paul' states: 'we...pray for you' (1.11); the
goal of his prayer is the mutual glorification of the Lord Jesus and
the congregation (1.12). At the beginning of part 3, he asks them:
'pray...for us' (3.1); the object of their prayer should be the
glorification of the word of the Lord (3.1).

Another structural feature of 2 Thessalonians as a whole consists in the carefully distributed occurrences of the word 'grace'. It
occurs – as usual – in the prescript (1.2), then at the end of part 1
(1.12), at the end of part 2 (2.16), and in the closing (3.18). In the
prescript, 'grace' is followed by 'peace' (1.2); just before the final
benediction with 'grace' (3.18), 'Paul' prays for 'peace' (3.16),
thereby creating a chiastic pattern in the beginning and end of the

letter (derived from 1 Thess. 1.1 and 5.23, 28; also in Rom. 1.7 and 16.20; 2 Cor. 1.2 and 13.11, 13; Gal. 1.3 and 6.16, 18; Eph. 1.2 and 6.23, 24).

Much of the above gives the impression that parts 1 and 3 belong together, and that part 2 stands out as the central one. This impression is shared by commentators, who generally recognize that the apocalyptic teaching of chapter 2 constitutes the main point of 2 Thessalonians; it is confirmed by a closer look at the content of the letter. Part 1 leads up to part 2, by introducing the theme of the eschatological retribution for present suffering at the parousia of Christ. Part 2 contains the warning against the idea that the day of the Lord is there. Part 3 draws the practical consequences from this warning, especially as far as the disorderly ones are concerned (we shall see later precisely how their behaviour is a consequence of their conviction that the day of the Lord is present).

At the beginning of part 1, we hear about the persecution of the congregation addressed in the letter (1.4); at the beginning of part 3, 'Paul' speaks about the opposition he has to face (3.1–2). Both times, the excellence of the congregation is brought out: 'Paul' boasts about them (1.4), and the word of the Lord is glorified among them (3.1).

In part 1, we hear about the actual conflict between the congregation and their persecutors that will be brought to a definite end 'at the revelation of the Lord Jesus', mentioned in the centre of this part (1.7). Part 3 is largely about the actual conflict within the congregation that is caused by the disorderly brothers and sisters; 'Paul' tries to bring it to an end by referring, in the centre of this part, to the example he has given in the past (3.7–10). In part 2, on the other hand, it is the conflict yet to come that is discussed: the apostasy and the activities of the 'man of lawlessness'. In the centre of this part, the author draws attention not to what will end the conflict, but to what delays its final outbreak: the restraining power or person (2.6–7). As the passage about this figure constitutes the centre of the central part of 2 Thessalonians, we may surmise that we have here the most important point of the message of the letter: the final outbreak of iniquity preceding the day of the Lord is not yet fully present, it is still inhibited by the restrainer.

In the following scheme, the most important observations of this section are summarized:

I (2 Thess. 1.3–12)	II (2 Thess. 2.1–17)	III (2 Thess. 3.1–16)
thanksgiving 1.3–4		prayer 3.5
prayer 1.11–12	prayer 2.16–17	prayer 3.16
'we...pray for you' 1.11		'pray...for us' 3.1
'grace' + 'peace' 1.2		
'grace' 1.12	'grace' 2.16	'peace' + 'grace' 3.16, 18
introductory thanksgiving	apocalyptic teaching	practical consequences
persecution of church 1.4		opposition to 'Paul' 3.1–2
actual conflict	future conflict	actual conflict

NUMERICAL ASPECTS OF THE STRUCTURE OF 2 THESSALONIANS

Two observations have to be added concerning the proportions in size between the three parts of 2 Thessalonians. In Antiquity (and also in later times), the size of a literary work and of its parts, and the proportions of size between these parts, were often considered to be an essential aspect of the structure of the work. Size could be measured in various ways: in lines of poetry, in words, in syllables, in verbal forms (see, e.g., Menken 1985; Smit Sibinga 1986, 1992). In counting in the text of 2 Thessalonians (i.e. in the Greek text as printed in the 26th edition of Nestle–Aland, with one correction; see my remarks on the English translation, pp. 7–8), I take the prescript together with part 1, and the closing with part 3, so that the three parts coincide with the chapters of the letter according to the traditional division.

We first look at the numbers of words. Part 1 has a size of 235 words, part 2 of 315 words, and part 3 of 274 words. This means that parts 1 and 2 together are practically twice as long as part 3 (550 and 274 words). More importantly, the proportion between part 2, on the one hand, and parts 1 and 3 together, on the other, is such that the proportion between the smaller segment (part 2, 315 words) and the larger segment (parts 1 and 3 together, 509 words) is equal to the proportion between the larger segment (509 words) and the whole (the entire letter, 824 words): $315 : 509 = 509 : 824$.

This division of a whole into two segments, so that the proportion between the smaller and the larger segment is equal to the proportion between the larger segment and the whole, is the so-called 'golden section', well known from classical mathematics.

Next, the numbers of verbal forms. Part 1 contains 25 verbal forms, part 2 has 46, and part 3 has 50. So part 3 contains exactly twice as many verbal forms as part 1. Here as well, we can make a more important observation. The proportion between part 2, on the one hand (46 verbal forms), and parts 1 and 3 together, on the other (75 verbal forms), corresponds again to a division according to the golden section: 46 : 75 = 75 : 121.

CONCLUSION

2 Thessalonians is a carefully constructed letter. All three parts of it display a concentric structure; the first and third parts belong together in various respects, and the second part stands out as the central one. Analysis of this composition may serve the exegesis of the letter in highlighting the central points of each part and of the letter as a whole, and in displaying correlations between corresponding elements.

Chapter 5

2 Thessalonians 1: Prescript and proem – the eschatological retribution

1.1–2: THE PRESCRIPT

The prescript of 2 Thessalonians has, as we saw, been borrowed from 1 Thessalonians; the author of the second letter only added a possessive pronoun, so that 'in God *the* Father' became 'in God *our* Father', and he added at the end the words 'from God our Father and the Lord Jesus Christ'. The former addition, a very simple one, concurs with the normal usage in both Thessalonian letters (1 Thess. 1.3; 3.11, 13; 2 Thess. 2.16). The latter addition constitutes an adaptation of the prescript of our letter to the standard form of the Pauline prescript (Rom. 1.7; 1 Cor. 1.3; 2 Cor. 1.2; Gal. 1.3; Eph. 1.2; Phil. 1.2; Philem. 3). If the author of 2 Thessalonians knew 1 Thessalonians, it is quite probable that he knew other letters of Paul as well.

At the beginning of **1.1**, the names of the three senders are simply put beside one another, without any qualifications: 'Paul, Silvanus, and Timothy'. It is clear in both letters that Paul is meant to be the principal one and the (real or fictitious) writer of the letter: his name is the first one in the prescript, and elsewhere in the two letters he appears as the sole author (1 Thess. 2.18; 3.5; 5.27; 2 Thess. 2.5; 3.17). Nevertheless, the first person plural is used very often in both letters; in 1 Thessalonians this may be considered, not as 'an epistolary plural', but as evidence of 'an intimacy of association in writing' (Frame 1912: 68), and the author of 2 Thessalonians imitates this usage.

Silvanus is the Latinized form of Silas, and that name is the Aramaic variant of the Hebrew name Saul (which was also Paul's own original Jewish name). According to Acts, Silas was one of the delegates of the Jerusalem church to communicate the decisions of the apostles and elders in Jerusalem to the church of Antioch (15.22–34), and he accompanied Paul on his so-called second missionary journey (15.40–18.22). He is also mentioned in 1 Peter 5.12. We hear in Acts that Timothy came from Lystra in Asia Minor, that he was the son of a Jewish mother and a Greek father, and that Paul circumcized him on account of the Jews living in Timothy's region (16.1–3); he accompanied Paul during the so-called second and third missionary journeys (15.40–21.16). Timothy is regularly mentioned in Paul's letters as Paul's co-worker, often entrusted with special tasks in the communication with churches (see, e.g., Rom. 16.21; 1 Cor. 4.17; 16.10; Phil. 2.19; 1 Thess. 3.2, 6), and he is the addressee of the (almost certainly Deuteropauline) letters to Timothy. Both co-senders were, according to Acts, with Paul during his visit to Thessalonica, when he founded a Christian community there (17.1–9), and on his stay in Corinth, when he wrote 1 Thessalonians (18.5; cf. 2 Cor. 1.19).

2 Thessalonians is – allegedly – addressed 'to the congregation of the Thessalonians in God our Father and the Lord Jesus Christ'. The Greek word *ekklēsia*, here translated as 'congregation', denotes a civic assembly. In the Septuagint (abbreviated as LXX), the old Greek translation of the Old Testament, it is a translation of the Hebrew word *qahal*, 'congregation', usually said of the congregation of Israel (see, e.g., Deut. 23.2–3). The earliest Christian community called themselves 'congregation of God' to indicate that they understood themselves as God's eschatological people (see, e.g., Gal. 1.13). In his undisputed letters, Paul uses *ekklēsia* almost always to refer to the local church (see, e.g., 1 Thess. 2.14; Gal. 1.2), and so it is used here, where it is qualified by 'of the Thessalonians', in imitation of 1 Thessalonians 1.1. The same usage is found in 2 Thessalonians 1.4. The addition 'in God our Father and the Lord Jesus Christ' is a necessary qualification, to delimit the Christian congregation from the Jewish or Gentile one. This congregation is within the sphere of authority of God and Christ.

God is qualified here and in 1.2 and 2.16 as 'our Father', all three times in formulaic language, as in 1 Thessalonians (1.1, 3; 3.11, 13). The formulaic language should not make us forget that for Paul, it is the experience of God's spirit that enables Christians to address God as 'Abba', 'Father', just as Jesus himself did (Rom. 8.15; Gal. 4.6; cf. Mark 14.36; see Roosen 1971: 23–4). For the writer of our letter, who locates himself in the Pauline tradition, it will have been the same. Jesus is called here 'Lord' and 'Christ'. The latter qualification means 'Anointed One' and is the Greek equivalent of 'Messiah'; in the Pauline and Deuteropauline letters, however, it is mostly used more as a proper name than as a title. Sometimes, though, Paul betrays that he is aware of the original meaning of the title (see, e.g., Rom. 9.5; 2 Cor. 5.10). We may surmise that the author of 2 Thessalonians knew that meaning as well, although it is not clearly present in his letter (at most in 3.5). The other qualification of Jesus, 'Lord', *kurios* in Greek, is, according to the pre-Pauline hymn in Philippians 2.6–11, God's own name, which he gave to Jesus when he exalted him at the resurrection (2.9–11). It indicates that Jesus holds sway, not only over his followers, but over the entire cosmos. It is often used by Paul, and for the author of 2 Thessalonians it is the favourite title to apply to Christ: he uses it twenty-two times in his short letter (see Trilling 1980: 57). This is not surprising: he is especially interested in Jesus' role as the exalted Lord, whose divine traits are more and more stressed, and who will return as the eschatological warrior to punish un-believers (1.7–9) and to annihilate the lawless one (2.8). The connection between the title 'Lord' for Jesus and his eschatological return traces back to the Aramaic-speaking church, as is evident from the Aramaic exclamation *Marana tha*, 'our Lord, come' (1 Cor. 16.22; *Didache* 10.6).

The names of senders and addressees are followed in **1.2** by the standard Pauline greeting formula: 'grace to you and peace from God our Father and the Lord Jesus Christ'. This formula, which may well have a liturgical origin, is not only a simple wish, that may or may not be realized; it is supposed that grace and peace really come on those to whom the words are addressed (for the efficacious function which was attributed to a greeting, see Matt. 10.12–13; Luke 10.5–6). 'Grace', *charis* in Greek, here denotes God's favour towards mankind, visible in his acts and especially, for Christians such as Paul and his followers, in what God did in Jesus (see, e.g., Rom. 3.24; 5.15). 'Peace', *eirēnē* in Greek, equivalent of the Hebrew *shalom*, is an inclusive indication of eschatological salvation (see, e.g., Zech. 9.10; Luke 1.79; Rom. 14.17). God's favour in Christ brings peace (cf. Luke 2.14).

God and Christ are then again mentioned as the sources of grace and peace. In this formula, they are apparently put on an equal level; in the light of the above, however, it seems to mean that God is the ultimate source of salvation, and Christ the one who has realized it. For Paul himself, this interpretation of the final words of

the greeting formula is supported by the long formula in Galatians
1.3–4: the simple formula is extended there by the addition to 'the
Lord Jesus Christ' of the words 'who gave himself for our sins to
deliver us from the present evil age, according to the will of our God
and Father'. The author of 2 Thessalonians, however, tends to put
Christ beside God (see 1.5–10, 12; 2.16; 3.5); this tendency concurs
with his view of Christ as the exalted Lord, who will gain eschatological victory.

1.3–4: THE THANKSGIVING

We have noted that 1.3–12 constitutes in fact one very long sentence, and the preceding analysis of the structure of the passage
may have given an idea of its internal coherence. It is only for
the sake of convenience that this one sentence is now, in the
commentary, broken up into various parts; the reader should not
forget that the thanksgiving ends in a description of eschatological
fulfilment, and is taken up in a prayer-report. In the entire proem,
the author reinforces his bonds with the addressees, and he introduces eschatology as the subject-matter of the letter in such a way
that already at the outset, the final salvation of the community is
stated as clearly as possible.

It was also noted above that in the Pauline and Deuteropauline
letters, the proem normally starts with a thanksgiving to or a
blessing of God, and that in the case of 2 Thessalonians, the
wording of the thanksgiving, which has much in common with
1 Thessalonians 1.2–3, has a somewhat formal ring about it: 'We
are *bound* to thank God always for you, brothers and sisters, *as
is fitting*' (**1.3**). Such expressions of obligation and appropriate-
ness point to a liturgical background; the author makes use of the
language of prayer (see Aus 1973). One should compare, for
instance, what the Jewish philosopher Philo of Alexandria (*c.* 15
BCE–*c.* 45 CE) says in his writing *On the Special Laws* 1.224: the
person who prospers in life, 'has as his bounden duty to requite
God his pilot...with hymns and benedictions and prayers and
sacrifices and the other expressions of gratitude as religion
demands' (trans. F. H. Colson, in Colson and Whitaker 1929–62,
vol. 7: 231).

The reason for the obligation to give thanks to God is that 'your
faith is strongly growing and the love of every one of all of you for
one another is increasing'. The community addressed here is, in

the view of the author, on the right path, in both the 'vertical' and the 'horizontal' dimensions of their Christian existence. 'Faith' is here their trust in God, the Father of Jesus Christ; our text presupposes of course the exposition of 1 Thessalonians 1.8–10, where the faith of the Thessalonians is said to be a 'faith in God', which is then explained as follows: 'how you turned to God from the idols, to serve the living and true God, and to await his Son from heaven, Jesus who saves us from the coming wrath'. 'Love' is here the very practical devotion of oneself to the other person, as praised by Paul in 1 Corinthians 13, considered by him as the fulfilment of the Torah (Rom. 13.8–10; Gal. 5.13–14). 'Hope', the third element of the triad in 1 Thessalonians 1.3, is missing here, but it returns under another term in the next verse, and is in fact essential to the entire letter.

The growth of the faith and love of the addressees has as its consequence that 'we ourselves boast about you among the congregations of God' (**1.4**). The motif of 'boasting' about the community comes from 1 Thessalonians 2.19. 'Boasting' is a favourite Pauline theme; the general tenor in Paul's use of it is that in the presence of God, humans have nothing to be proud of, unless of what God did for them or through them (see, e.g., 1 Cor. 1.27–31; the quotation from Jer. 9.24, with which this passage ends, shows that the concept has Old Testament roots). In 2 Corinthians 10–12, the theme of boasting is very prominent; over against opponents who boast of their own qualities and achievements, Paul paradoxically boasts of his weaknesses, in which God's power becomes visible. When Paul boasts of his churches (as in 1 Thess. 2.19; 2 Cor. 9.2–3), he does not boast of his own achievements, but of what God has done in the believers (cf. 2 Cor. 1.12).

That is also what happens in 2 Thessalonians 1.4: 'Paul' boasts of his addressees among 'the churches of God' (these are not specified), and he does so 'for your steadfastness and faith under all your persecutions and under the oppressions you endure' (a comparable content is found in 1 Thess. 1.6–8). The concept of hope, missing in 1.3, appears here in its practical consequence: 'steadfastness' (*hupomonē* in Greek; cf. 1 Thess. 1.3). It is the attitude of patiently waiting, often in distressing circumstances, for God to realize fully the salvation he has begun in Christ (see esp. Rom. 5.2–6; 8.24–5). In our text, 'steadfastness' is coupled to 'faith' (*pistis* in Greek), because 'steadfastness' is the aspect of faith that is most important under the present circumstances. For Paul, 'faith' and 'hope' are intimately connected, as he shows with the example of Abraham, 'who believed against hope in hope, that he would become the father of many nations' (Rom. 4.18; cf. 15.13; Gal. 5.5; Col 1.23). The combination of 'faith' and 'steadfastness' in 2 Thessalonians 1.4 may have been influenced especially by 1 Thessalonians 1.9–10, where 'faith in God' has been said to imply awaiting his Son from heaven.

The addressees of 2 Thessalonians are enduring 'persecutions' and 'oppressions'; these two concepts denote here almost the same thing, the former being the more specific (the latter concept is found in 1 Thessalonians 1.6; 3.3–4,7). What follows in 2 Thessalonians 1.5–7, and also what is said in 2.7,15–17; 3.3, 5, strongly suggests that persecution and oppression indeed mark the situation of the addressees, although details about it are not given. 'Oppression', *thlipsis* in Greek, is a concept that is at home in apocalyptic eschatology. The oppression of God's faithful is supposed to reach its apogee just before the end. This period of extreme tribulation is often called the time of the 'messianic woes', preceding the appearance of the Messiah. In Daniel 12.1, we hear that 'there will be a time of oppression, as there has not been since there was a nation till that time, and at that time your people will be delivered, all those who will be found written in the book'. The same thought is found in the Qumran *War Scroll* (1.11–12; 15.1). In *2 Baruch* 24.3–4, Baruch asks God about the sign of the end. God answers him (25.2–4):

> This then will be the sign: When horror seizes the inhabitants of earth, and they fall into many tribulations and further, they fall into great torments. And it will happen that they will say in their thoughts because of their great tribulations, 'The Mighty One does not anymore remember the earth'; It will happen when they lose hope, that the time will awake.
>
> (trans. A. F. J. Klijn, in Charlesworth 1983: 629)

In what follows (chs 26–30), the various coming calamities are described in detail; after them, the Messiah will appear. We encounter the same ideas in Christian apocalyptic eschatology: Jesus announces in the 'synoptic apocalypse' that, just before the parousia of the Son of Man, there will be days of unprecedented oppression (Mark 13.19, 24 and parallels), and in Revelation 7.14, the multitude before God's throne are said to be 'those who have come out of the great oppression'. The author of 2 Thessalonians interprets, as it seems, the persecutions and oppressions which the addressed community is experiencing, as somehow related to the events preceding the end; from what follows in 1.5–10, it is evident that their present sufferings will end soon. It is also evident, that *in* the situation of persecution, some members of the congregation became convinced that Christ's parousia had occurred (2.1–2); that is only possible when the present affliction was seen as an anticipation of the end. It will become clear from what follows, however, that it is not considered by our author as part of the end itself.

1.5–10: THE ESCHATOLOGICAL RETRIBUTION AT THE REVELATION OF THE LORD JESUS

The connection between 1.4 and **1.5** is not immediately clear: to what do the words 'a token of God's just judgment' at the beginning of 1.5 refer? The simplest and most obvious solution is that they refer to the persecutions and oppressions mentioned at the end of 1.4; these are said to constitute evidence of God's righteous judgment. The idea of a divine judgment is a very general religious idea, also found in Old and New Testaments (see, e.g., Deut. 10.17–18; Rom. 2.1–16); in apocalyptic eschatology, God's judicial activities are logically concentrated in his final judgment, as we saw in *1 Enoch* 1. The main question concerning 2 Thessalonians 1.4–5 is: how can persecutions and oppressions be evidence of God's just judgment? The answer is to be found in a theological reasoning, current in the environment of our author, according to which the present sufferings of God's people are God's punishment for their sins, so that afterwards, at the final judgment, they will not have to be punished with the wicked but will participate in God's salvation (see Bassler 1984). In the *Psalms of Solomon*, a Jewish collection of poems from the first century BCE, we read:

> For the Lord will spare his devout,
>   and he will wipe away their mistakes with discipline.
> For the life of the righteous (goes on) forever,
>   but sinners shall be taken away to destruction,
>   and no memory of them will ever be found.
> But the Lord's mercy is upon the devout
>   and his mercy is upon those who fear him.
>   (13.10–12; trans. R. B. Wright, in Charlesworth 1985: 663)

The same idea is found in *2 Baruch* 13.8–10. After Baruch has seen the capture of Jerusalem by the Babylonians, God says to Baruch, who will 'be preserved until the end of times' (13.3), what he has to tell the cities of the nations, when they inquire about the why and when of God's eschatological retribution:

> You who have drunk the clarified wine,
> you now drink its dregs,
> for the judgment of the Most High is impartial.
> Therefore, he did not spare his own sons first,
> but he afflicted them as his enemies because they sinned.
> Therefore, they were once punished,
> that they might be forgiven.
>
> (trans. A. F. J. Klijn, in Charlesworth 1983: 625)

The present oppression of the community is thus evidence of God's just, impartial judgment, and at the same time of their election: they are enduring oppression now in order to 'be deemed worthy of the kingdom of God, for which you are suffering'. Because they are chastized now, God will finally deem them worthy of his kingdom, of entering the space where God really exerts his royal power; the expression 'the kingdom of God' is here used as an encompassing indication of eschatological salvation (cf. 1 Thess. 2.12).

By interpreting the present situation of the congregation in this way, the author of the letter introduces in his proem the main theme of his writing, the coming of the day of the Lord. As stated above, part of the community thought in their present distress that the day of the Lord had come; this point of view is refuted already implicitly in 1.5: their present suffering shows that they are still being chastized by God in order to be saved on that day. The author of 2 Thessalonians is trying here, within his eschatological frame of thought, to make sense of the present negative experiences of his community and of himself.

He continues, in **1.6–7a**, with an explanation of God's just judgment: 'since indeed it is just in God's eyes to repay those who oppress you with oppression, and you who are oppressed with liberation together with us'. This is the ancient *lex talionis*, the law of retribution, known from Exodus 21.23–5 and similar passages ('an eye for an eye, a tooth for a tooth...'), but now transposed to the level of divine, eschatological retribution, as also happens in Matthew 7.1–2 and Luke 16.25, for instance. Those who are presently oppressing the congregation will be oppressed by God in the coming age, and the oppressed congregation will then find 'liberation', another term for the coming salvation (cf., e.g., Acts 3.20). They will do so together with 'us', that is, with 'Paul, Silvanus and Timothy' (1.1), who identify themselves with the suffering community (cf. also 3.2). 'To repay' is a current designation of God's judicial action, found in, for example, Deuteronomy 32.35, which passage is quoted in the New Testament in Romans 12.19 and Hebrews 10.30. A passage that is especially important in view of 2 Thessalonians 1.6, is Isaiah 66.6: 'The voice of the Lord who repays repayment to his enemies'. This text resembles, in wording and content, the verse under consideration; we shall see, moreover, that Isaiah 66 has exerted a strong influence on the following description of the parousia of Christ (see Aus 1976: 263–8; according to Aus 1977, Isaiah 66 would also have influenced 2 Thessalonians 2.6–7, but that is difficult to demonstrate).

In **1.7b–8a**, the author mentions the moment of the retribution: the revelation (*apokalupsis*) of the Lord Jesus. In the Greek text, there follows, in 1.8b–10, a participial clause which governs a series of subordinate clauses; in my translation, it has become a temporal subordinate clause ('when he will mete out...'), with appended clauses. The complex of 1.8b–10 depicts again the eschatological retribution. Its style is marked by synonymous parallelism: each clause is made up of two parallel halves; the second half repeats the thought of the first half in cognate terms (so in 1.8, 9, 10). The wording of the entire passage 1.7b–10 is heavily reminiscent of Old Testament passages; we already saw that this is a characteristic feature of apocalyptic eschatology. The passage also resembles, of course, other texts in the field of apocalyptic eschatology (a list of parallels from the Old Testament and from other Jewish literature can be found in Rigaux 1956: 624). So it is clear that the author is here drawing on traditional materials, as happens so often in the field of apocalyptic eschatology. In comparison with what has preceded in 1.5–7a, there is a significant change: now 'the Lord Jesus' is the subject of the retribution. This shift is easily understood in a letter in which Jesus is preferably called 'the Lord': he bears God's own name and exercises God's functions, among them the office of eschatological judge.

The Lord Jesus will be revealed 'from heaven': as we saw earlier, he is, in the early Christian view, since his resurrection with God in

heaven, and is expected to return from there (1 Thess. 1.10; 4.16; 1
Cor. 1.7; 1 Pet. 1.7, 13). The revelation is not the revelation of the
secrets of the heavenly world to the apocalyptic visionary, but the
public realization of the ultimate secret: the coming of the saviour.
By coming from heaven, Jesus acts just as God does (see, e.g., Is.
63.19). The same is valid for the next qualification of his coming:
'together with the angels of his might'. The angels are God's
heavenly court or host, accompanying him when he comes for
judgment (see, e.g., Zech. 14.5; *1 Enoch* 1.9); in early Christianity,
the returning Christ is attended by them (as in Mark 8.38; *Didache*
16.7). They are called 'the angels of his might', because they serve
him in exercising his eschatological task: so the returned Christ
sends his angels out to gather the elect, according to the 'synoptic
apocalypse' (Mark 13.27 and parallel). Jesus' revelation is qualified
in the third place as occurring 'in flaming fire'. Fire belongs to the
standard elements of a theophany: God's revelation to Moses in the
burning bush takes place 'in flaming fire' (Exod. 3.2), and Daniel
sees in his vision that God's throne is 'flaming fire' (Dan. 7.9), to
mention just two familiar Old Testament examples. Fire is also the
element with which judgment is executed (see, e.g., Ps. 50.3; 1 Cor.
3.13, 15), and that may very well be meant here, not only because of
what follows (Christ punishing unbelievers), but also because the
expression 'in flaming fire' has been derived here probably from
Isaiah 66.15 in agreement with the general interest of our author in
Isaiah 66. In this verse, God is said to 'pay back his anger in fury, and
his rebuke in flaming fire', and in the following verse he is said to
execute judgment upon all flesh by fire.

The influence of Isaiah 66.15 is also perceptible in what follows
in 2 Thessalonians **1.8**: 'when he [Christ] will mete out punishment
to those who do not know God and to those who do not obey the
gospel of our Lord Jesus'. In the LXX of Isaiah 66.15, the Hebrew
word translated above by 'anger' is rendered by *ekdikēsis*, 'punishment', also used in 2 Thessalonians 1.8. This verse has been
influenced by Isaiah 66.4 as well: God says there that he will
'repay' to the wicked the things they dread, 'because I called and
no one answered'; for the Hebrew verb translated by 'answer', the
LXX has the Greek verb *hupakouein*, 'to obey', which is also used in
2 Thessalonians 1.8. We observe once more that Isaiah 66 (in the
LXX version) has been one of the sources of inspiration of the
author of 2 Thessalonians. Isaiah 66 can be read as a description of
God's eschatological salvation of the righteous and punishment of

the wicked, and in that quality it was used and esteemed in early Christianity (Is. 66.1–2 is quoted in Acts 7.49–50; for other examples, compare Rev. 12.2, 5 with Is. 66.7; John 16.22 with Is. 66.14; 2 Pet. 3.13 and Rev. 21.1 with Is. 66.22; Mark 9.48 with Is. 66.24).

In the words 'those who do not know God', we can recognize Jeremiah 10.25: 'Pour out your fury upon the nations who do not know you' (cf. Ps. 79.6; the same allusion occurs in 1 Thess. 4.5). As the word 'nations' is absent in 2 Thessalonians 1.8, there is no reason to make the words just quoted from this verse refer to the Gentiles, nor is there reason to make 'those who do not obey the gospel of our Lord Jesus' refer to Jews only (in 1 Thess. 4.5, on the contrary, the Gentiles are explicitly mentioned). Israel can be said not to know God (Jer. 9.2, 5), and Gentiles can be said not to obey the gospel (Rom. 10.16). Both indications concern the oppressors mentioned in 1.6; for our author, who, as we saw, considers Jesus as bearing God's name and exercising God's functions, rejection of the gospel, the good news of Jesus, is tantamount to a refusal of God himself ('to know' has here a strong, existential meaning, cf., e.g., Jer. 31.34; John 10.14–15).

The idea that God is just and thus punishes the wicked is widespread; we find it in Old Testament passages such as Deuteronomy 32.35 (quoted in the New Testament in Rom. 12.19; Heb. 10.30; see above); Ezekiel 25.14, 17 and in New Testament passages such as Luke 21.22; 1 Peter 2.14. In apocalyptic eschatology, God's punishment or revenge is part of the theodicy: those who oppressed God's people in this age, will be punished in the coming age (see, e.g., Rev. 6.10; 19.2).

In **1.9**, the punishment is explained; it is 'the penalty of eternal destruction, far away from the Lord and from the glory of his power'. 'Eternal' here simply means that the penalty is temporally unlimited. The word 'destruction' is not uncommon for God's final punishment of his foes (see 1 Thess. 5.3; 1 Tim. 6.9; Phil. 1.28; 3.19). In *Psalm of Solomon* 2.31, God is said to 'put to sleep the arrogant for eternal destruction in dishonor, because they did not know him' (trans. R. B. Wright, in Charlesworth 1985: 654). In 2 Thessalonians 1.9, the destruction does not amount to a total annihilation; it consists in being excluded from the company of the Lord – the reversal of the Pauline idea that the final salvation consists in 'being with the Lord' or 'living with the Lord' (see 1 Thess. 4.17; 5.10; 2 Cor. 13.4; Phil. 1.23). Paul does not depict the salvation of the coming age in expressive terms; the language he uses to describe that which is not yet, is rather sober. The same applies to the author of 2 Thessalonians in his description of the fate of the wicked; he does not draw a graphic image of the tortures of hell, but reduces the picture to its bare essence: their exclusion from the presence of the Lord. The same restraint characterizes his words on the salvation of believers in 1.10, and on the events of the end in 2.1–12.

The final words of 1.9 are, in a literal translation: 'far away from the face of the Lord and from the glory of his power'. They have been derived from Isaiah 2.10, 19, and 21. Isaiah 2.6–22 is a description of God's judgment of 'the house of Jacob' (2.6); such a text could be read easily as dealing with God's final judgment, and the borrowing from it in 2 Thessalonians 1.9 occurred no doubt on the presupposition that it indeed concerns the events of the end. Three times we hear in the Isaiah passage that people will hide themselves (I translate again literally) 'far away from the face of the terror of the Lord and from the majesty of his highness'. The LXX has 'far away from the face of the terror of the Lord and from the glory of his power', and this version has been used in 2 Thessalonians. In Hebrew the word 'face' is often used re-dundantly in combination with a preposition in cases where we would use a preposition only: in Isaiah 2.10, 19, and 21 we would simply say 'far away from the terror of the Lord'. The LXX translates this Hebrew idiom literally, here and in many com-parable instances. Now the author of our letter omits 'of the terror', probably because after God's final judgment there is no question any longer of people seeking to hide themselves from God's terror. The omission, however, has the result that the word 'face' regains something of its proper meaning: 'far away from the face of the Lord' is equivalent to 'far away from the presence of the Lord', which can be translated simply as 'far away from the Lord' (so also von Dobschütz 1909: 249–50). In Isaiah, 'the Lord' is God (the Greek word *kurios* translates the Hebrew name of God *Jhwh*), but in 2 Thessalonians 1.9 it is Christ, who has been mentioned in the two preceding verses as 'the/our Lord Jesus'. We have again an example of the creative use of an Old Testament passage in Christian apocalyptic eschatology.

'Glory' (*doxa* in Greek) is the splendour which belongs to God and which he has given to the risen Christ (1 Pet. 1.21). Here it is intimately associated with the power of Christ, just as he is said to return 'with great might and glory' in the 'synoptic apocalypse'

(Mark 13.26 and parallels). According to 2.14, believers will participate in the glory of Christ; this theme is also touched upon in the next verse, 1.10, and made explicit in 1.12.

We meet in **1.10** a temporal subordinate clause which specifies once more the point in time of the retribution of 1.6–7a. After the indications 'at the revelation of the Lord Jesus...' and 'when he will mete out...', that moment is now referred to as: 'when he comes on that day to be glorified in his saints and to be admired in all who have believed'. At the same time, the verse contrasts with the preceding verse: the fate of the faithful is opposed to the fate of the unbelievers. The words 'on that day' are in Greek at the end of the verse, so that they have a certain emphasis: they round off that part of the long sentence of 1.3–12 that started with 'at the revelation of the Lord Jesus' (1.7) and they announce the theme of the next section of the letter.

The 'coming' of God or his eschatological agent, and 'that day' as an indication of the time this coming will occur, are normal elements of apocalyptic eschatology (see, e.g., Zech. 9.9, 16; Mal. 3.1–2; also in the 'synoptic apocalypse', Mark 13.26, 32 and parallels). Here 'on that day' may be linked especially with Isaiah 2.11, 17, and 20. The goal of the coming of the Lord is indicated with two infinitives, both of them determined by a prepositional phrase, and the whole constitutes a synonymous parallelism: 'to be glorified in his saints and to be admired in all who have believed'. Both halves of the parallelism are, again, allusions to Old Testament texts. In the LXX, Psalm 88.8 (Psalm 88 in the LXX counting is Psalm 89 in the counting of the Hebrew text) reads: 'God being glorified in the council of the saints', and the LXX version of Psalm 67(68).36 has: 'God is admired in his saints' (in both Psalm verses, the Hebrew is slightly different). In both instances, 'the saints' (or 'holy ones') are angels. In 2 Thessalonians 1.10, the parallelism of 'his saints' and 'all who have believed' strongly suggests that Christians are meant. In Paul's letters, 'the saints' are almost always the Christians (see, e.g., 2 Cor. 1.1; Phil. 4.22; a possible exception is 1 Thess. 3.13, to be compared with Zech. 14.5). The image of God with his angels is transferred to Christ with his church.

The preposition 'in' has here primarily the meaning of 'among', 'in the presence of', as was also the case in the two psalm verses quoted above: while the presence of the Lord will be denied to the persecutors, the believing community will enjoy it (cf. 1 Thess.

4.17). Second, there may be also the idea that the Lord is glorified and admired *in* the believers who participate in his glory (cf. 1.12; 2.14; Rom. 8.18; Phil. 3.21). The glory of the Lord will be visible in them (cf. Is. 49.3).

At the end of the verse, 'Paul' returns so to speak from the eschatological bliss to the reality of the present, with the parenthetical clause 'because our testimony to you was believed'. The clause shows that the addressed community is supposed to belong to 'all who have believed'. The community has believed the testimony of the sender of the letter, a testimony which is identical to 'the gospel of our Lord Jesus Christ' (1.8). For our author, belief in the gospel is what distinguishes in the present the oppressed from the oppressors, and in the future the elect from the damned. The depiction of the future fates of believers and unbelievers is in black and white, without nuances. We have to realize that it serves to encourage the addressees to remain steadfast in their distress and to stay within the community of believers, and such a goal in such a situation does not leave much room for fine distinctions.

1.11–12: THE PRAYER-REPORT

The return to the present is continued in the prayer of the sender for the Christian life of the congregation. It is not an actual prayer, but, as usual in a letter, a report of the steady prayer of the sender (probably inspired by 1 Thess. 1.2), and it takes up, in both form and content, the thanksgiving of 2 Thessalonians 1.3–4 (see the analysis of the structure of the letter). It is connected with what precedes: 'To this end we always pray for you' (**1.11**). The words 'to this end' refer to the final salvation of the believers set out in what immediately precedes.

Both the fact that 'Paul' prays for the church and the content of the prayer show that the salvation of the congregation is not something that will take place automatically. The first part of the content of the prayer is 'that our God may deem you worthy of the calling'. 'The calling' refers to the activity of 'our God' (an indication which suits a prayer), who invited them through the preaching of the gospel 'to the community with his Son Jesus Christ our Lord' (1 Cor. 1.9). That relationship implies a share in the coming age which God has inaugurated in Jesus, so that in 1 Thessalonians 2.12 Paul can speak of 'God who called you to his kingdom and glory' (cf. 4.7), and 'Paul' can say in 2 Thessalonians

2.14 that God 'called you through our gospel, so that you may obtain the glory of our Lord Jesus Christ'. God's calling also implies a 'holy' way of life (1 Thess. 4.7). In 2 Thessalonians 1.11, the sender asks God that at the final judgment, God may consider the addressees worthy of the invitation which he extended to them, and which they accepted at their conversion (cf. 1.5).

In the second part of the content of the prayer, the author states the condition for God's deeming the congregation worthy of the call: that God 'may mightily bring to fulfilment every good resolution and work of faith'. God will complete, by his power, what the members of the congregation have begun. In the description of what they do, there is a progression from 'every good resolution' to 'work of faith'; 'Paul' starts with the intention, and ends with the execution. 'Work of faith' (derived from 1 Thess. 1.3) refers to the practical aspect of faith; one can think of the love and the steadfastness mentioned in 2 Thessalonians 1.3–4. It is presupposed here that, in the good that Christians are willing and doing, God is working. One might speak of a double causality: both the Christians themselves *and* God's Spirit are working. This idea is also found in Paul's genuine letters – for instance, in Philippians 2.12–13: 'Work out your own salvation with fear and trembling; for it is God who works in you both the willing and the working beyond your resolve' (cf. Rom. 8.4). Anyhow, it is the congregation's own responsibility, sanctified by the Spirit (cf. 2 Thess. 2.13), to work in order to be deemed worthy of their calling; their participation in the coming age will not come about as a matter of course. The hortatory section at the end of the letter (3.1–16) is announced here.

The goal of their and God's action is 'that the name of our Lord Jesus may be glorified in you, and you in him' (**1.12**). This phrase echoes Isaiah 66.5; in that verse, the LXX translation has the clause 'that the name of the Lord be glorified'. Again, words about God as the Lord are applied to 'our Lord Jesus'. We meet here the same verb 'to glorify' as in 1.10. In that verse, it was used in parallelism with 'to admire', and consequently, it had to mean 'to honour', 'to praise'. However, the verb can have the stronger meaning 'to give splendour', 'to make glorious'. In 1.12, the meaning of the verb inclines in the latter direction, because the glorification now has a mutual character: the glorification of the addressees in Christ does not mean that they are honoured 'in his name' or 'in him', but has to mean that they participate in the glory, the divine splendour of the risen Christ; this participation was already suggested in 1.10 (see above) and will be mentioned again in 2.14. The preposition 'in' can then retain the usual local meaning it also had in 1.10, but this time with a mystical ring: the name of the Lord acquires glory *in* the believers, and they acquire glory *in* him. 'The name of our Lord Jesus' hardly differs from 'our Lord Jesus', since in a context such as this one, name and person are all but identical: a name is what is manifest of a person. In 3.6, 'Paul' commands 'in the name of our Lord Jesus Christ', and in 3.12 he does the same 'in the Lord Jesus Christ'.

The point in time of the mutual glorification of the Lord and his church is not indicated. On the basis of the context, a reference to both the future and the present can be argued. Verse 1.10 suggests the former, 1.11 the latter. It may well be that the author wants his readers to understand both things: in the present Christian life of the community the mutual glorification has already begun, and it will be completed in the full glory of Christ and the faithful in the coming age. This is the thought expressed by Paul in 2 Corinthians 3.18: 'While we behold with unveiled face the glory of the Lord, we are all being transformed into the same image, from glory into glory, as by the Lord who is Spirit' (cf. Rom. 8.30).

The mutual glorification is said to happen 'according to the grace of our God and the Lord Jesus Christ'. These words echo the initial greeting (1.2) and connect the future salvation, which is already operative in the present, with its source, the favour of God and Christ. The final words of 1.12 confront us with an interesting problem: does the author of 2 Thessalonians consider Jesus as God? The Greek words translated above as 'of our God and the Lord Jesus Christ' can also be translated as 'of our God and Lord Jesus Christ' (the Greek text has only one definite article, before 'God'). There are, indeed, in some New Testament writings that are generally considered as late (that is, dating from the end of the first or the beginning of the second century), passages in which Jesus is unequivocally called 'God' (John 20.28; Tit. 2.13; 2 Pet. 1.1). If 2 Thessalonians is a Deuteropauline letter, written around the end of the first century, it is quite possible that Jesus is called 'God' here. The transfer to Jesus, in this letter, of divine attributes and of Old Testament passages about God could also concur with such an interpretation of 1.12. Nevertheless, when our author mentions Jesus and God in the same breath (see, apart from 1.12: 1.1, 2; 2.16), he distinguishes between them, and nowhere else does he straightforwardly call Jesus 'God'. So it seems probable that the ambiguous phrase at the end of 1.12 has arisen as a result of the awkward combination of two formulae. In Greek, 'of our God' has an article, because it follows a substantive with an article ('the grace'; cf., e.g., 1 Cor. 3.10). The author has then appended the phrase 'and of the Lord Jesus', without a definite article in Greek, as it is usual in 2 Thessalonians (1.1, 2; 3.12). Thus there is no compelling reason to suppose that he calls Jesus 'God'.

Chapter 6

2 Thessalonians 2: The body of the letter – the day of the Lord has not yet come

2.1–3a: THE WARNING THAT THE DAY OF THE LORD IS NOT YET PRESENT

With the phrase 'we beg you, brothers and sisters' (**2.1**), 'Paul' marks the transition to the body of the letter. His request to the community concerns 'the coming of our Lord Jesus Christ and his gathering of us to himself', two topics that are very closely united (they have only one definite article in Greek). 'Coming' is here the translation of the Greek word *parousia*, a term that was in use in the Hellenistic world to designate 'the visit of a human ruler or a high official to a city, with appropriate ceremonies being held and honors being bestowed, or of the visit of a god to an individual or to cultic followers' (Wanamaker 1990: 125). Early Christians applied the word to Jesus' eschatological coming in glory (see, e.g., Matt. 24.27, 37, 39; Jas. 5.7, 8). Paul too employs the word in this pregnant sense, especially in 1 Thessalonians (2.19; 3.13; 4.15; 5.23; further 1 Cor. 15.23), and our author borrows it from that letter.

The other topic, 'his gathering of us to himself', is also a well-known eschatological theme. In the Old Testament, various prophetic sayings can be found on God gathering his scattered people from their exile (e.g., Is. 27.13; 43.4–7; Jer. 31.8). Later, God is expected to gather Israel for final salvation (e.g., 2 Macc. 2.7, 18; Sir. 36.10); in its Christian version, this expectation concerns the church, as in the prayer in *Didache* 10.5: 'Remember, Lord [God], your church...and gather it from the four winds into your kingdom, which you prepared for it'. The task of gathering God's people can be transferred to God's eschatological agent. We read, for instance, about the Messiah in *Psalm of Solomon* 17.26, 28: 'He will gather a

holy people whom he will lead in righteousness....He will distribute
them upon the land according to their tribes' (trans. R. B. Wright, in
Charlesworth 1985: 667). In the 'synoptic apocalypse', Christ is the
one who gathers the elect through his angels (Mark 13.27 and
parallel). In 2 Thessalonians 2.1, Christ is said to gather us 'to
himself'; the personal meeting between Christ and the believer is
again hinted at, as in 1.9–10 and 12.

The content of the request is put forward in **2.2**. As suggested
above, this verse contains the main point of the letter, and to
understand it correctly is pivotal to an understanding of the letter
as a whole. The verse begins with a double indication of what the
addressees should not do: 'Do not rashly lose your senses and do
not be alarmed'. They are apparently in danger of being upset, but
they should not lose their common sense, and not be shocked. Both
kinds of mental agitation are caused by the message that the day of
the Lord is present, and may therefore denote both rapture about
the coming of salvation and fear of judgment; these states of mind
can be found at the same time in the same person. The warning
'not to be alarmed' occurs also in the 'synoptic apocalypse', in
connection with hearing of wars and rumours of wars (Mark 13.7
and parallel). To impress it upon the addressees, the warning is
repeated in somewhat different words at the beginning of **2.3**: 'Let
no one deceive you in any way'. This clause explicitly brands as
deceit the message that the day of the Lord has come. In the
'synoptic apocalypse', Jesus' followers are repeatedly warned not to
be 'led astray' by 'false Christs' or 'false prophets' (Mark 13.5–6 and
parallels; Matt 24.11; Mark 13.22 and parallel).

In what follows in 2 Thessalonians 2.2, three sources of agitation
are mentioned: 'either by a prophetic utterance or by a word or by
a letter purporting to be from us'. In the chapter on the author of
2 Thessalonians, I have already explained that the words 'purporting to be from us' have to apply at least to 'a letter', and that a
part of 1 Thessalonians (4.13–5.11), interpreted in such a way that
it supported the conviction that the day of the Lord had come, is
probably in view. It is reasonable to suppose that 'purporting to be
from us' applies to 'a word' as well, because in 2.15 Paul's word and
letter (again 1 Thessalonians is meant) are mentioned together as
the means of transmission of the traditions to which the addressees
have to hold fast. 'A word...purporting to be from us' in 2.2 refers
then also to Paul's oral teaching. It is hard to tell whether
'purporting to be from us' bears also on the prophetic utterance;

anyhow, a prophetic saying is not mentioned in the corresponding verse 2.15.

The message which should not disturb the congregation, and for which people are falsely appealing to Paul, is 'that the day of the Lord has come'. We have to dwell on the meaning of this phrase at some length, on account of both its importance within 2 Thessalonians and the divergence of the interpretations that have been given to it. It has been supposed that the belief that 'the day of the Lord has come', should be interpreted as an early form of Gnosticism. 'Gnosticism' can be circumscribed in this case as a type of Christianity in which salvation is achieved by knowledge (*gnōsis* in Greek); this knowledge concerns the heavenly origin and destination of the spiritual element in human beings. The conviction that 'the day of the Lord has come' would then be comparable to the belief rejected in 2 Timothy 2.18, 'that the resurrection has already taken place': the Gnostics have already attained final salvation by their knowledge (see especially Schmithals 1965: 138–53; for Hughes 1989: 84–95, the error mentioned in 2 Thess. 2.2 is a Pauline *gnōsis* such as that contained in Ephesians and Colossians). The point is, however, that the wording both of the eschatological error in 2.2 and of its rebuttal in 2.3–12 suggests not Gnosticism but apocalyptic eschatology – at least in the perception of the author of 2 Thessalonians. What would be the sense of attacking a Gnostic error by means of an apocalyptic exposition about what has to happen before the arrival of 'the day of the Lord'? If the author of 2 Thessalonians intended to combat a belief that the resurrection had already taken place in a spiritual form, we should expect something other than what we do have in 2 Thessalonians 2 (so also, e.g., Best 1972: 276–7). It seems then that we have to look for ideas in the field of apocalyptic eschatology to answer the question as to what the eschatological error in 2 Thessalonians 2.2 precisely implies.

It is now almost universally acknowledged that the Greek clause at the end of the verse should be translated as: 'The day of the Lord is present, has come' (see Stephenson 1968). Though the translation 'The day of the Lord is imminent' might be theoretically possible, it is virtually excluded for our text by the circumstance that with that translation the statement in question would lose the 'heretical' character it should have according to its context: it does not essentially differ then from what Paul states in Romans

13.11–12 and Philippians 4.5 (cf. 1 Thess. 4.15–17; 5.1–11; 1 Cor. 7.29; 15.52), and what other New Testament authors state as well (Mark 1.15; Jas. 5.8; 1 Pet. 4.7; Rev. 1.3; 22.10), namely, that the end is impending. Many scholars choose the translation: 'The day of the Lord has come', but then interpret it as if it was actually: 'The day of the Lord is imminent' (e.g., von Dobschütz 1909: 267–8; Stephenson 1968: 451); such a policy, however, does not recommend itself, as it also deprives the statement of the content it needs in its context. It is not very probable that the author of 2 Thessalonians, who uses Paul's name for his work, combats a statement that Paul himself could easily have made. Moreover, the author of our letter himself is convinced that the final decision is at hand, though not yet immediately. He writes about the things that have to happen before the parousia will actually occur, and which are already working in the present time: 'For the mystery of lawlessness is already at work' (2.7).

However, if we translate in 2.2: 'The day of the Lord has come', we are left with the question what exactly this statement may have implied. Some scholars interpret it in this way: it cannot mean that the parousia has already occurred, for that should be a public event, perceptible for everybody, leaving no room for doubt; so it can only mean that the chain of events which eventually lead up to the parousia has begun (e.g., Frame 1912: 248; Trilling 1980: 79). Now this interpretation has as its main problem that, in the idiom of the author of 2 Thessalonians and of Paul, 'the coming (*parousia*) of the Lord' and 'the day of the Lord' refer to the same event. It is obvious that in 2 Thessalonians 2.2 the expression 'the day of the Lord' takes up the earlier 'the coming of our Lord Jesus Christ and his gathering of us to himself' (2.1); the point made here is that the addressees should not think about this event, that it has already occurred. In 1 Thessalonians 4.15 and 5.2, there is no need at all to suppose different referents for the two expressions, and the same applies to 1 Corinthians 1.8; 5.5 and 15.23. Moreover, Paul can make almost identical statements about 'the coming of the Lord' and 'the day of the Lord': compare 1 Corinthians 1.8 and Philippians 1.10 with 1 Thessalonians 3.13 and 5.23 (the congregation shall be blameless at the coming/on the day of Christ/the Lord) or Philippians 2.16 with 1 Thessalonians 2.19 (the congregation will constitute Paul's boast on the day of Christ/at his coming). It is true that the parousia as described in 2 Thessalonians 2 is unmistakable; it is quite possible, however, that not all Christians in the first century saw it precisely that way, or considered the same events as unmistakable, so that the supporters of the view that 'the day of the Lord has come', may have perceived the parousia of Christ in a way different from that of the author of the letter (cf. Trilling 1972: 126).

Our problem remains: what exactly did the statement 'the day of the Lord has come' imply for its adherents as the author of 2 Thessalonians understood them? In view of the fact that – as observed above – the expression 'the day of the Lord' in 2.2 takes up 'the coming of our Lord Jesus Christ and his gathering of us to himself' from 2.1, it is obvious that 'the day of the Lord' implies some personal appearance of the Lord, who will assemble his faithful. Such a conception of 'the day of the Lord' is in line with the conception the author of 2 Thessalonians himself has of this day, as is evident from 1.7–10 (see above, pp. 87–92); 2.8 (about the Lord, who will kill the lawless one and destroy him 'by the manifestation of his coming'). It should be noticed here that our author does not give any evidence that he calls in question the *character* of 'the day of the Lord' as viewed by his opponents; he only discusses its *timing*. Apparently some real, personal presence of the Lord is envisaged.

To get things still clearer, it is again the 'synoptic apocalypse' (Mark 13 and parallels) that can be of help. It displays several similarities with the eschatological passage 2 Thessalonians 2.1–12 (see Rigaux 1956: 95–105; Hartman 1966: 195–205; Holland 1988: 134–42); apparently, both come from the same world of thought. In the 'synoptic apocalypse' Jesus is presented as warning against those who will say that they are the Christ, false Christs and false prophets who will lead people astray. In all three synoptic gospels, Jesus starts the discourse with a warning against 'many', who will come in his name, saying: 'I am he' (Mark 13.6; Luke 21.8), or 'I am the Christ' (Matt. 24.5). The deceivers pretend to be Christ returned on earth. In Matthew's version of the discourse, we meet another reference to 'false prophets' leading many astray in 24.11. 'False Christs' and 'false prophets' are again mentioned in Mark 13.22 and its parallel Matthew 24.24; they will perform signs and wonders to lead astray, if possible, the elect. In the preceding verse (Mark 13.21; Matt. 24.23), the listeners are admonished not to believe those who pretend to be able to indicate the place where the Christ is (cf. also Matt. 24.26; Luke 17.23). The most reasonable explanation for all these warnings is that there were indeed people who claimed to be or were supposed to be the eschatological prophet or Christ returned on earth, at least at the time Mark's Gospel was composed (*c.* 70 CE). On the Jewish side, we have very specific testimonies about such persons in the stories which the historian Flavius Josephus (*c.* 37–100/110 CE) tells us about those who passed themselves off as prophets who were on the point of realizing eschatological salvation for their followers. I quote two examples:

> At this time [= *c.* 54 CE] there came to Jerusalem from Egypt a man who declared that he was a prophet and advised the masses of the common people to go out with him to the mountain called the Mount of Olives, which lies opposite the city at a distance of five furlongs. For he asserted that he wished to demonstrate from there that at his command Jerusalem's walls would fall down, through which he promised to provide them an entrance into the city.

> Festus [procurator of Palestine, *c.* 60–2 CE] also sent a force of cavalry and infantry against the dupes of a certain impostor who had promised them salvation and rest from troubles, if they chose to follow him into the wilderness.
>
> (*Jewish Antiquities* 20.169–70, 188; trans. L. H. Feldman,
> in Thackeray *et al.* 1926–65, vol. 9: 481, 491)

Again, we can observe evident parallels between 2 Thessalonians 2.1–12 and the 'synoptic apocalypse'. According to the latter, the endtime is introduced by, among other things, the appearance of people claiming to be Christ returned on earth, and by persecution of the Christian community (Mark 13.9–13 and parallels), which events are not yet the end (Mark 13.7 and parallels). According to the former there are, at the time of the writing of 2 Thessalonians, which is marked by persecution of the church (1.4), persons who claim that the parousia has taken place (2.2); the author rebuts this claim by pointing to future events that have to take place before the parousia (2.3–12).

I conclude that the phrase 'the day of the Lord has come' (2 Thess. 2.2) meant for its adherents, as understood by the author of 2 Thessalonians, that Christ had already returned on earth and was already performing his task, or was on the point of doing so.

2.3b–5: THE APOSTASY AND THE REVELATION OF THE MAN OF LAWLESSNESS, THE SON OF PERDITION

In **2.3b**, the author of 2 Thessalonians mentions two events that have to happen before the coming of the day of the Lord: 'For that day will not arrive, unless the apostasy comes first and the man of lawlessness is revealed, the son of perdition, who opposes and exalts himself against every so-called god or object of worship, so that he takes his seat in the temple of God, declaring himself to be God'. This long sentence is an anacoluthon, a sentence that has no proper end; the Greek equivalent of the words 'that day will not arrive' at its beginning are actually missing in the original text, but they constitute a necessary logical complement.

The time adjunct 'first' bears on both the apostasy and the revelation of the lawless one. It is not suggested that the former precedes the latter; the two events are in fact quite closely related. There is no new time adjunct 'then' or 'later' connected with the revelation of the man of lawlessness, and in 2.9–12 the coming of the lawless one is said to occur with deceit and delusion for those who perish. We shall also see that the conduct of Antiochus Epiphanes as described in Daniel constitutes a background to both events.

The definite article in '*the* apostasy' and '*the* man of lawlessness' shows that the addressees are supposed to be familiar with both entities. Both of them indeed belong to the usual elements of apocalyptic eschatology. When we studied the milieu of 2 Thessalonians (see pp. 59–63), we already saw that the apostasy occurs, in various forms, in early Jewish and early Christian apocalyptic eschatology. It is found in an ancient text such as *1 Enoch* 91.5–7 where Enoch says:

> For I know that the state of violence will intensify upon the earth; a great plague shall be executed upon the earth; all (forms of) oppression will be carried out; and everything shall be uprooted; and every arrow shall fly fast. Oppression shall recur once more and be carried out upon the earth; every (form of) oppression, injustice, and iniquity shall infect (the world) twofold. When sin, oppression, blasphemy, and injustice increase, crime, iniquity, and uncleanliness shall be committed and increase (likewise).
>
> (trans. E. Isaac, in Charlesworth 1983: 72)

We meet the idea of the eschatological apostasy of part of God's people in Daniel, where the Syrian King Antiochus Epiphanes is considered as its instigator (see Dan. 8.24–5; 9.27; 11.23, 30–5; in 1 Macc. 2.15, the effect of the measures of this king is called 'apostasy'). In the *Commentary on Habakkuk* from Qumran (in which the prophetic text is applied to persons and circumstances in the time of the commentator, which time is considered as the time of the end), Habakkuk 1.5 is interpreted as referring to 'the unfaithful together with the man of lies' (2.1–10).

All these parallels, and also 2 Thessalonians 2.9–12, show that the apostasy of 2 Thessalonians 2.3 is a religious phenomenon with ethical implications. It is clear that the apostasy from the Torah as meant in Daniel is easily enlarged into a more general kind of defection. In 2 Thessalonians 2.10–12, it is described in such general terms as 'not accepting the love of the truth', 'believing what is false', 'not believing the truth' and 'having pleasure in sinfulness'. The subject of the apostasy is not specified, and there is no reason to exclude Christians from the danger of defection. The apostasy to come should be distinguished from the situation at the time of writing of 2 Thessalonians, in which apparently some from the congregation are erring (2.2; 3.6–15). Nevertheless, the present error foreshadows the coming apostasy, because 'the mystery of lawlessness is already at work' (2.7); we saw that in the same way the present persecution was considered as an anticipation of the end (1.4). The author of 2 Thessalonians sees the congregation as standing on the threshold of the events of the end: what they are experiencing at present is not yet the great oppression and apostasy of the end, but it constitutes, so to say, the preamble to these events.

The other event to occur before the day of the Lord is the revelation of the man of lawlessness. This person, evidently a human being, will be revealed, just as the Lord Jesus will be (1.7). Jesus will come from heaven; it is not said where the man of lawlessness will come from. The expression 'the man of lawlessness' is a Semitism, just as the other qualification of the same person: 'the son of perdition'. In such constructions, 'man', 'son' and the like are used with a following noun in the genitive to express a quality. So, 'the man of lawlessness' (*ho anthrōpos tēs anomias* in Greek) means 'the lawless one' (*ho anomos* in Greek), as he is called in 2.8, and 'son of perdition' means 'one who brings perdition' or 'one who will suffer perdition' (cf. Ps. 89.23, where the LXX speaks of a 'son of lawlessness', and John 17.12, where Judas receives the epithet 'son of perdition'). 'Lawlessness' does not indicate here absence of law, but transgression of law. The law in question is not so much the Mosaic Torah as the Christian 'truth' (2.10, 12, 13), found in the gospel (1.8; 2.14). The perdition which the lawless one will suffer is depicted in 2.8: the Lord Jesus will kill and destroy him. 'Perdition' is one of the possible designations of the horrible final fate of the wicked (cf. 2 Pet. 3.7).

In **2.4**, the man of lawlessness is further qualified: he is an anti-God figure with divine claims. 'Paul' picks up the tradition of the 'tyrant of the endtime'; this figure constitutes a human personi-fication of the evil that increases just before the end. The tradition of the 'tyrant of the endtime' was actualized in an influential way in Daniel's depiction of Antiochus Epiphanes, but not only there (see Jenks 1991: 153–68, 175–83). The lawless one is here described as 'who opposes and exalts himself against every so-called god or object of worship'. This wording is reminiscent of what we read in Daniel 11.36–7:

> And the king will do according to his will, and he will exalt and magnify himself against every god, and against the God of gods he will speak outrageous things....And to the god of his fathers he will not pay attention, nor to the darling of women [probably Tammuz; see Ezek. 8.14]; to any other god he will not pay attention, for against all he will magnify himself.

This passage concerns the activities of Antiochus Epiphanes as narrated in 1 Maccabees 1.16–64, but now considered, within an apocalyptic perspective, as the outburst of eschatological evil. 'Paul' does not exactly quote from Daniel, but the allusion cannot be missed. He introduces a significant change: 'against every god, and against the God of gods' becomes 'against every so-called god'. The change looks like a correction from the point of view of mono-theism (so also Dibelius 1937, on 2 Thess. 2.4). The visionary of Daniel seems to accept the existence of pagan gods, who are subordinate to the God of Israel, and he denounces King Antiochus for not acknowledging any god at all, neither his own pagan gods nor Israel's God. For the author of 2 Thessalonians, on the other hand, the pagan gods do not really exist, but are only called 'gods', and at the same time the wording is broad enough to include the one God (who will be mentioned in the next clause): the lawless one is opposing everything that human beings call 'god', either rightly or wrongly. To emphasize his utterly anti-God posture still more, it is added that he also opposes every 'object of worship'. Nothing is sacred to the lawless one.

His anti-God attitude goes so far 'that he takes his seat in the temple of God, declaring himself to be God'. 'The temple of God' refers to the temple in Jerusalem; it is clear that, following an 'object of worship', a material temple has to be in view, and only in a material temple does it make sense to say that a human being 'declares himself to be God'. The historical events in the background of these words also suggest that the Jerusalem temple is meant.

First of all, in 169–167 BCE King Antiochus Epiphanes plundered the temple of Jerusalem and abolished the temple service; the temple was made into a temple of Zeus Olympius (2 Macc. 6.2) or *baal-shamem*, 'the lord of heaven', and an altar for this deity was built on the altar of burnt offering. On account of such acts, Antiochus Epiphanes is qualified, in Daniel 11.36–7, as opposing every god; in Daniel 9.27; 11.31 and 12.11, the suppression of the cult is mentioned, and the altar for *baal-shamem* is called, in a play on words, *shiqquṣ shomem*, 'the abomination of desolation' (cf. 1 Macc. 1.54, and also Mark 13.14; Matt. 24.15). Antiochus Epiphanes as interpreted in Daniel is clearly one of the historical figures who have served as a model for the lawless one taking his seat in the temple.

Another one is the Roman general Pompey, who took Judea in 63 BCE; after the capture of Jerusalem, he entered the Holy of Holies in the temple. These events are reflected in *Psalm of Solomon* 17.11–15, in wording which is similar, in several respects, to 2 Thessalonians 2.3–4, 8–12:

The lawless one laid waste our land....
As the enemy (was) a stranger
   and his heart alien to our God, he acted arrogantly.
So he did in Jerusalem all the things
   that gentiles do for their gods in their cities.
And the children of the covenant (living) among the gentile rabble
   adopted these (practices).
No one among them in Jerusalem acted (with) mercy or truth.
                    (trans. R. B. Wright, in Charlesworth 1985: 666)

The third historical figure behind the description of the lawless one in 2 Thessalonians 2.4 is the Roman Emperor Gaius Caligula (37–41 CE). Josephus' account is quite clear:

> The insolence with which the emperor Gaius defied fortune surpassed all bounds: he wished to be considered a god and to be hailed as such, he cut off the flower of the nobility of his country, and his impiety extended even to Judaea. In fact, he sent Petronius with an army to Jerusalem to instal in the sanctuary statues of himself.
>
> (*Jewish War* 2.184–5; trans. H. St J. Thackeray, in Thackeray *et al.* 1926–65, vol. 2: 395)

It was only due to Petronius' common sense and Caligula's death that the statues were in fact never set up.

It is true that none of the three historical figures just mentioned has actually been 'sitting in the temple of God, declaring himself to be God', but it is only a small step from their actions to the action of the lawless one in 2 Thessalonians 2.4, a step that is easily taken by someone who is reflecting on these past models of human arrogance in the light of expected eschatological evil. Moreover, the Old Testament provided examples of kings who were supposed to have made themselves equal to God. According to Isaiah 14.13–14, the king of Babylon said in his heart:

> To heaven I shall ascend,
>   above the stars of God
> I shall exalt my throne,
>   and I shall dwell on the mountain of assembly [of the gods],
> in the far regions of the north.
> I shall ascend to the heights of the clouds,
> I shall make myself like the Most High.

In Ezekiel 28.2, similar assertions are put into the mouth of the ruler of Tyre. Mention should also be made here of the expectation of a return of the Roman Emperor Nero. He died in 68 CE, and soon after his death rumours arose that he had not died but had fled to Parthia, from where he would return to Rome. One Jewish text in which this expectation is reflected is the fifth book of the *Sibylline Oracles*. The *Sibylline Oracles* are a collection of Jewish and Christian oracles attributed to the pagan Sybil. In the (Jewish) fifth book, dating from the period 80–132 CE, we find a passage about Nero in which his lawlessness and his divine pretensions (evident

from, among other things, his attempt to dig a channel through the
Isthmus of Corinth) are prominent:

> ...who one day
> will lay hands on his own family and slay them, and throw
>   everything into confusion,
> athlete, charioteer, murderer, one who dares one thousand
>   things.
> He will also cut the mountain between two seas and defile it
>   with gore.
> But even when he disappears he will be destructive. Then he
>   will return
> declaring himself equal to God. But he will prove that he is not.
>   (5.29–34; trans. J. J. Collins, in Charlesworth 1983: 393)

Nero never had direct dealings with the temple in Jerusalem,
although the fact that the Jewish War began in his reign was reason
enough for the one who wrote *Sibylline Oracles* 5.150 to say of
Nero: 'He seized the divinely built Temple' (trans. J. J. Collins, in
Charlesworth 1983: 396). It will be clear that to presuppose that
Nero is one of the many figures who have coalesced into the figure
of the man of lawlessness as drawn in 2 Thessalonians 2.3–4, is only
possible if we date 2 Thessalonians to some time between the year
80 and the early second century CE, as suggested above (see p. 66).

In that case, the temple of Jerusalem no longer existed at the
time of writing of the letter. The mention of the temple in 2.4 has to
be explained as part of the fiction created by the pseudonymous
author, who knew very well that the temple still stood during
Paul's apostolic career. We should also keep in mind, that in Greek
the clause 'so that he takes his seat in the temple of God' does not
necessarily indicate the actual event. 'Paul' is only expressing, in
the strongest possible way, the arrogant anti-God attitude of the
lawless one: he will be capable of occupying God's earthly abode,
and taking God's place.

In **2.5**, 'Paul' refers to his earlier oral teaching: 'Do you not
remember that I told you these things when I was still with you?'
The Greek imperfect tense of 'I told' suggests that the teaching on
the eschatological apostasy and the revelation of the man of
lawlessness was given on more than one occasion. A statement
such as this also belongs, of course, to the pseudonymous fiction,
and it seems to have been derived from 1 Thessalonians 3.4. We
should not forget that, for our author, 2 Thessalonians constitutes

an authentic application of Pauline tradition (including Paul's oral teaching) to the situation in which 1 Thessalonians had been used to support the conviction that the day of the Lord had come. Verse 2.5 also serves, as we saw above, as a transition to the next topic: after the reference to his past teaching, 'Paul' turns to the present knowledge of his addressees.

2.6–7: THE RESTRAINING POWER OR PERSON

When we studied the structure of 2 Thessalonians, we saw that verses **2.6–7** are in the centre of the central part of 2 Thessalonians, and we surmised that they constitute the most important point of the letter. At the same time, these two verses are very difficult to translate and to interpret. They run as follows: 'And now you know what restrains him, so that he will be revealed at his own time. For the mystery of lawlessness is already at work, only until the one who restrains now will have disappeared'.

A comparison of this translation with other, extant translations may give an impression of the various possibilities of rendering this passage. A full discussion of its various grammatical and lexicographical problems would become too technical (see for such a discussion Barnouin 1977); a few notes are nevertheless necessary. In general, my translation has the advantage that it does not presuppose complicated constructions or ellipses (i.e. omissions of words); it is based on the most simple and straight-forward reading of the Greek text. An ellipsis is often assumed in 2.7b; putting a comma between 2.7a and 7b results, in my view, in a reasonably smooth and complete sentence (cf. Best 1972: 294). (In ancient manuscripts, there is hardly any punctuation; punctuation marks in modern editions and translations are insertions by the editor or the translator.)

In a passage that concerns the timing of the events of the end, the adverb 'now' at the beginning of 2.6 can be supposed to have its normal temporal sense. It qualifies 'you know'; the present knowledge of the addressees is primarily contrasted with the author's teaching when he was still with the congregation (2.5), and secondarily with the future revelation of the lawless one ('and then the lawless one will be revealed', 2.8). The clause 'so that he will be revealed at his own time' cannot be connected with the verb 'to know', but it links up well with the verb 'to restrain'. The words 'he' and 'his' in this clause have to refer to the man of lawlessness:

his revelation is also mentioned immediately before and after the passage under consideration, in 2.3, 8. To translate the Greek verb *katechein* as 'to restrain' is one possibility out of several (other possible translations are, for instance, 'to hold sway' or 'to possess'). The translation 'to restrain' or something similar is suggested in this case by the following clause 'so that he will be revealed at his own time': these words show that the revelation of the lawless one will take place at a definite, predetermined time, and is impossible before that time. It is also suggested by the opposition, in 2.7–8, between the present hidden, mysterious activity of lawlessness, and its future overt outbreak; 2.7b shows in the above translation (which is, as I said, the most simple and obvious one) that the transition from hidden to open activity occurs precisely when the figure whose activity is described with the verb *katechein* disappears from the scene. There is apparently something or somebody that at present still obstructs the revelation of the lawless one, and this figure seems to be on the side of God, as it obstructs the final outbreak of iniquity. We shall see, moreover, that such an obstructing factor, directed by God, is not uncommon in the thought world of apocalyptic eschatology. So it seems best to adopt the translation 'to restrain'. This option implies that the man of lawlessness is the object of 'to restrain'. In the Greek text, the verb has no object, neither in 2.6 nor in 2.7; in my translation, I have supplied, for the sake of clarity, the pronoun 'him' in 2.6. A peculiar feature of 2.6–7 is that the restraining entity is indicated in the Greek text in 2.6 by a neuter participle ('the restraining thing', 'the restraining power'), and in 2.7 by a masculine participle ('the restraining person'). This feature of the text demands an explanation. On both occasions, the author of the letter puts the participle earlier in the clause than one would normally expect it; in that way, he gives it a certain emphasis.

When we try to interpret 2.6–7, we should start from the presupposition that the author of the letter expected to be understood by the addressees. His reminding of earlier teaching in 2.5 does not mean that what he writes in 2.6–7 is totally new; the words 'and now you know' strongly suggest that the addressees have knowledge about the point to be dealt with, either also from teaching or from familiarity with apocalyptic eschatology. However, for us, as modern readers of 2 Thessalonians, it is much more difficult to find out what 'Paul' wants to say here.

In the course of history, many answers have been brought

forward to the question who or what is behind the restraining power or person (see, e.g., Trilling 1980: 94–102). A few examples should be discussed. Since the Church Fathers Hippolytus and Tertullian, at the beginning of the third century CE, it has often been thought that the restraining power was the Roman Empire, and the restraining person the Roman Emperor. This political interpretation finds no support in the text of 2 Thessalonians; it breaks down on the evident lack of interest, on the part of our author, in the reality of the historical Roman state. As far as 'Paul' betrays any interest in kings or emperors (see above, on 2.3–4), he is only interested in their religious role.

A much more probable interpretation has been given by A. Strobel (see Strobel 1961: 98–116). He has shown that in early Judaism and in early Christianity the prophecy of Habakkuk 2.3 was considered as important proof for God's total control of the events of the end. God determines the time of the end; the delay of the end (or what looks like delay in human perception) is also according to God's plan. A clear and early specimen of this interpretation of Habakkuk 2.3 is found in the *Commentary on Habakkuk* of the Qumran sect (the text of Hab. 2.3 has been italicized):

> *For there shall be yet another vision concerning the appointed time. It shall tell of the end and shall not lie.*
> Interpreted, this means that the final age shall be prolonged, and shall exceed all that the Prophets have said; for the mysteries of God are astounding.
> *If it tarries, wait for it, for it shall surely come and shall not be late.*
> Interpreted, this concerns the men of truth who keep the law [i.e., the members of the Qumran sect], whose hands shall not slacken in the service of truth when the final age is prolonged. For all the ages of God reach their appointed end as He determines for them in the mysteries of His wisdom.
> (7.5–14; trans. G. Vermes 1975: 239)

In early Christian literature, we meet a similar reading of Habakkuk 2.3 in Hebrews 10.35–9, and, with an emphasis on God's indulgence, in 2 Peter 3.8–9. Strobel interprets 2 Thessalonians 2.6–7 against this background: the restraining power is the plan of salvation, established by God, and the restraining person is God himself. A great advantage of Strobel's interpretation of 2 Thessalonians 2.6–7 is that he tries to understand this passage on the basis

of early Jewish and early Christian testimonies that are contemporary with 2 Thessalonians. His view is not without prob-
lematic aspects. Direct influence of Habakkuk 2.3 is not discernible
in 2 Thessalonians 2.6–7, so that it may be preferable to say that
both early Jewish and early Christian interpretations of Habakkuk
2.3, and passages such as 2 Thessalonians 2.6–7, are based on
the conviction that God alone is the Lord of history, and that
he alone determines when the end will come. Strobel's identifica-
tion of the restraining person with God himself breaks down on
2.7b: it is inconceivable that God is said to disappear from the
scene. Such a statement can be made about emissaries of God,
but not about God himself.

A different solution for the riddle of the restraining power or
person in 2 Thessalonians 2.6–7 has been proposed by C. H. Giblin
(see Giblin 1967: 166–242, and also Giblin 1990). He translates
the Greek verb *katechein* as 'to possess', 'to seize'; he considers
the 'seizing power' as a pseudo-prophetic force, and the 'seizing
person' as a pseudo-prophet, whose activity is part of the mystery of
lawlessness, that will be consummated in the appearance of the
man of lawlessness. The activity of the pseudo-prophet is the cause
of the disturbance in the congregation depicted in 2.1–2; 3.6–12. It
is indicated in 2.7b that the lawless one will be revealed when the
pseudo-prophet has been removed from the community. Apart
from some linguistic problems, Giblin's thesis is improbable in that
it blurs the apparent function of the power or person indicated by
the verb *katechein*: to block the revelation of the lawless one. When
it or he has this function, it or he has to be not on the side of the
lawless one, but on God's side. Another improbable aspect of
Giblin's theory is that the removal of a pseudo-prophet from one
specific community would be the condition for the revelation of the
lawless one.

To arrive at a correct understanding of 2.6–7, we should take
into account not only the evidence of the text itself suggesting that
the restraining power or person is on God's side, but also the
conviction generally found in apocalyptic eschatology and discussed above, that God controls history and determines the time
of the end. It may seem that in the present time Satan and his
adherents have the final word, but in reality God is in charge.
Satan and his followers only have power as long as God allows
them to have it. In the Book of Revelation, it is repeatedly said that
the power to do evil 'was given' to various supernatural figures

(see, e.g., 6.4, 8; 7.2; 13.5, 7, 14, 15); the passive form 'was given' is an instance of the 'theological passive', a circumlocution used to avoid naming God as the agent. In the *Apocalypse of Abraham*, Abraham has a vision of Adam and Eve and Satan, called here Azazel, in Paradise; Abraham and God have this conversation on Azazel:

> And I [Abraham] said, 'Eternal, Mighty One, why then did you adjudge him such dominion that through his works he could ruin humankind on earth?' And he [God] said to me, 'Hear, Abraham! Those who desire evil, and all whom I have hated as they commit them – over them did I give him dominion, and he was to be beloved of them.'
> (23.12–13; trans. R. Rubinkiewicz, in Charlesworth 1983: 700–1)

In 2 Thessalonians 2.11–12, Satan's activity is ultimately reduced to God's work. Taking all this into account, we may consider the restraining power of 2.6 to refer to the plan or the will of God. God has decided at what time it will be given to the lawless one, who is an instrument of Satan (2.9), to be revealed.

According to 2.7a, 'the mystery of lawlessness is already at work'. Lawlessness is already present in a hidden way in what the community is experiencing. In apocalyptic eschatology, the mysteries of creation and of history are with God in heaven; they include what will become reality at the end of history. In *1 Enoch* 103.2–3, Enoch says to the righteous ones:

> For I know this mystery; I have read the tablets of heaven and have seen the holy writings, and I have understood the writing in them; and they are inscribed concerning you. For all good things, and joy and honor are prepared for and written down for the souls of those who died in righteousness.
> (trans. E. Isaac, in Charlesworth 1983: 83)

In the writings of the Qumran sect, 'mysteries' are frequently mentioned (see, e.g., *Commentary on Habakkuk* 7.8, quoted above), including 'the mysteries of his [Belial's] animosity', which did not turn the members of the sect away from God's covenant (*War Scroll* 14.9). Even these mysteries are, of course, within God's control. Along the same lines, 'the mystery of lawlessness' of 2 Thessalonians 2.7 belongs to the secrets to be revealed at the end (2.8); God allows its influence to be felt already in the present.

This situation will continue 'only until the one who restrains now will have disappeared' (2.7b). As observed above, 'the one who restrains now' cannot be God himself, but it has to be somebody through whom God is active in restraining the lawless one. Most probably, 'Paul' aims at an angel who has a function comparable to the angel of Revelation 20.1–3, who keeps Satan in confinement for a thousand years, or to the angel of Revelation 9.13–15, who is ordered to release the angels of doom. When this angel disappears, in agreement with God's plan, then the lawless one will be revealed. So 'the one who restrains now' executes 'what restrains him', that is, God's plan (so also, e.g., Holland 1988: 110–13; Müller 1988: 50–1).

I finally note that reading 2.7 as one sentence gives a natural sense to the conjunction 'for' at its beginning: the lawless one will be revealed, according to God's plan, at the predetermined time, because God has set a temporal limit to the activity of the angel who now restrains him. In fact, 'for' mainly connects the second half of 2.6 with the second half of 2.7: the disappearance of the restraining angel is the explanation for the revelation of the lawless one.

2.8–12: THE REVELATION AND ANNIHILATION OF THE LAWLESS ONE, AND HIS LEADING ASTRAY OF THE UNBELIEVERS

'Paul' has ended the passage on the cause of delay in the manifestation of the lawless one with an announcement of the disappearance of the restrainer; 'and then' at the beginning of **2.8** refers to that moment, which has already been qualified, in 2.6, as 'his own time'. When the restrainer has disappeared, 'the lawless one will be revealed'. The secretly working 'mystery of lawlessness' is followed by its overt outbreak. The thought of 2.3–4, and the reference to it at the end of 2.6, are now resumed.

The first thing we hear about the lawless one is the elaboration of his title 'the son of perdition' from 2.3, in the relative clause 'he whom the Lord Jesus will kill with the breath of his mouth and destroy by the manifestation of his coming'. Somewhat illogically, his end is described before his coming, which follows in 2.9–10. An effect of this illogical sequence is, that the reader or hearer of the letter is fortified in his trust in the final victory of the Lord Jesus, and that beforehand the sting is taken out of the actions of the lawless one as depicted in the following verses.

The actual description, in a synonymous parallelism, of the

defeat of the lawless one contributes to this effect. The first half of the parallelism is based on Isaiah 11.4, a fragment from the prophecy on the 'shoot from the stump of Jesse' (Is. 11.1–9): 'He [the coming king] will strike the earth with the rod of his mouth, and with the breath of his lips he will kill the wicked'. This text has evidently been influential in apocalyptic eschatology; it was read as a prophecy on the final victory of God's agent in the eschatological holy war. We find testimonies not only in Revelation 19.15, 21, but also in, for instance, *4 Ezra* 13.10: 'I [Ezra] saw only how he ['the man from the sea', God's agent] sent forth from his mouth as it were a stream of fire, and from his lips a flaming breath' (trans. B. M. Metzger, in Charlesworth 1983: 551). Isaiah's parallelism has been contracted, in 2 Thessalonians, to 'killing with the breath of his mouth'. This phrase suggests that the lawless one will not withstand the slightest activity on the part of the Lord Jesus: the latter has only to breathe to kill the former. The contraction may have been influenced by the wording of Psalm 33.6, where it is said that God made 'the host of heavens' 'by the breath of his mouth'. If this text is in the background, then we have here again an instance of the transfer of divine predicates to Jesus.

The second half of the parallelism contains a picture of Jesus' activity which is still more powerful: he will not only kill the lawless one, but he will 'annihilate' him (cf. 1 Cor. 15.24, 26). He will do so 'by the manifestation of his coming'. The words 'coming' (Greek *parousia*; see above, in the comments on 2.1) and 'manifestation' (Greek *epiphaneia*) are virtually synonymous. The latter term indicated in the Hellenistic world the salvific appearance of a god, which can take place in a king (Antiochus Epiphanes means 'Antiochus, god manifest'). It is used in writings such as 2 Maccabees, where it indicates the appearance from heaven of Israel's God on behalf of his people (see, e.g., 2.21; 3.24), and the Pastorals, where it refers to the final coming of Christ (see, e.g., 1 Tim. 6.14; Tit. 2.13). The expression 'the manifestation of his coming' is somewhat clumsy, unless *epiphaneia* has the meaning of 'sudden manifestation'; in that case, it contributes to the impression of Christ destroying the enemy without any effort. 'The manifestation of his coming' must of course parallel 'the breath of his mouth' in the preceding clause.

In a second relative clause, the coming of the lawless one is pictured: 'the one whose coming takes place by virtue of the work of Satan with all power and false signs and wonders and with all sinful deceit, for those who perish' (**2.9–10a**; 'takes place' is a 'futuristic present', just as 'sends' in 2.11). We already observed in the commentary on 2.3, that both the lawless one and Jesus have a 'revelation'. It now appears that just like the Lord Jesus, the lawless one has a 'coming' (*parousia*), and has the power to perform 'signs and wonders'. And just as Jesus worked by virtue of the Spirit of God (see, e.g., Matt. 12.28), so the lawless one works 'by virtue of the work of Satan'. His activity is a parody of that of Jesus; the moving spirit behind it is Satan. 'Satan' originally means 'adversary' or 'accuser' (see, e.g., 1 Kings 11.14); it especially denotes a celestial being that accuses humans before God (see Job 1.6–2.7; Zech. 3.1–2). In 1 Chronicles 21.1, he appears as a seducer. He becomes the chief of the fallen angels, the great adversary of God and his people (see, e.g., *1 Enoch* 54.6). In the New Testament also, he is the great seducer, the enemy of God, Jesus and the faithful (see, e.g., Mark 1.13; 4.15; Luke 13.16; 22.3; Rom. 16.20; Rev. 12.9).

The lawless one, instrument of Satan, who has been described in 2.4 as an anti-God figure, is now depicted as a false prophet, who causes the apostasy mentioned in 2.3. His coming is accompanied by 'all power and false signs and wonders', just as the false Christs and false prophets, who will arise before the coming of the Son of Man, will perform 'great signs and wonders' to lead astray the elect, according to the 'synoptic apocalypse' (Mark 13.22 and parallel). It seems that 'Paul' (and the author of Revelation, see Rev. 19.20) compresses into one person the evil that the 'synoptic apocalypse' ascribes to a series of human beings. In view of the connection with 'signs and wonders', it seems logical to consider 'power' primarily as the capacity to perform miracles (cf. Rom. 15.19). 'Signs and wonders' is a standard combination, already in the Old Testament (see, e.g., Exod. 7.3; Deut. 6.22; Acts 2.22, 43). In our text, they are qualified as 'false', literally 'of lie' or 'of falsehood' (*pseudos* in Greek): falsehood is the source and the effect of these miracles. They are real miracles, but they are intended to lead people astray, just as Israel's false prophets led the people astray (see esp. Deut. 13.2–6; Jer. 23), and the eschatological false prophet or prophets try to lead the church astray (see above).

The aspect just touched on (the effect the false prophet has on people) is explicitly mentioned at the beginning of 2.10: 'with all sinful deceit', literally 'with all deceit of sinfulness'. 'Sinfulness' or 'unrighteousness' (Greek *adikia*) is a very general term to indicate iniquity; it is obvious that along with similar terms, it is used to describe the evil of the last days (see, e.g., *1 Enoch* 91.5–7, quoted above in the commentary on 2.3). It is almost a commonplace of apocalyptic eschatology that, just before the end, God's adversary or adversaries will successfully deceive people. I have already referred to the activities of the eschatological false prophet(s). According to Daniel 8.25, King Antiochus Epiphanes 'will successfully practise deceit with his own hand'. In *Sibylline Oracles* 3.64–70, a passage probably more or less contemporary with 2 Thessalonians, it is said about Beliar, i.e. Satan:

> ...he will raise up the height of mountains, he will raise up the sea,
> the great fiery sun and shining moon,
> and he will raise up the dead, and perform many signs
> for men. But they will not be effective in him.
> But he will, indeed, also lead men astray, and he will lead astray
> many faithful, chosen Hebrews, and also other lawless men
> who have not yet listened to the word of God.
>   (trans. J. J. Collins, in Charlesworth 1983: 363)

Again, signs and deceit go hand in hand. I also refer to *Didache* 16.4, a passage discussed in the chapter on the milieu of 2 Thessalonians, where we hear of 'false prophets and corrupters', who will appear in the last days, and where the eschatological adversary is called 'the deceiver of the world', who 'will appear like the son of God and perform signs and wonders'.

The words 'for those who perish' are best connected with what immediately precedes: the deceit of the lawless one. His signs and wonders are of course perceptible for everyone, but the deceit inherent in them and his other misleading activities achieve their aim only with 'those who perish'. The present tense suggests that the future doom of 'those who perish' is already operative in the present (cf. 2.7). 'Paul' here primarily thinks of those who are at present oppressing the congregation (cf. 1.5–10); he has explained in 1.9 how he understands their perdition: in the end they 'will suffer the penalty of eternal destruction, far away from the Lord and from the glory of his power'.

The perdition of 'those who perish' is a consequence of their own choice: they perish 'because they did not accept the love of the truth so as to be saved' (**2.10b**). They had the chance 'to be saved' (Greek *sōzein* means 'to save'), which is the opposite of 'to perish' (cf. also 1 Cor. 1.18; 2 Cor. 2.15). 'The truth' (*alētheia* in Greek) is a very broad concept, but in 2 Thessalonians it has in fact the restricted meaning of the *Christian* truth, that is, the gospel. We have already seen in 1.8, 10, that the oppressors 'do not obey the gospel of our Lord Jesus', whereas the congregation did believe 'our testimony to you', and in 2.13–14, we shall hear of their 'belief in the truth', which is tantamount to answering to God's calling 'through our gospel'. The same usage of 'the truth' for 'the gospel' occurs in Paul's genuine letters (2 Cor. 4.2; 6.7; Gal. 5.7; cf. Gal. 2.5,14). It rests on the presupposition that in the Christian gospel the ultimate truth about God and humankind is revealed. The reproach to the unbelievers is not that they did not accept the truth, but that 'they did not accept the love of the truth'. This peculiar expression can be explained by the view our author has of God's rule of everything, a view that clearly emerges in the next verse, where God is said to send 'a power that works delusion'. It is God who gives to human beings the ability to accept the gospel. At the same time, however, they themselves remain responsible for their decisions: they refused to accept this gift from God. We meet here the negative side of the double causality that we observed in 1.11. The author uses a past tense ('they did not accept') to show that from his perspective the decision not to accept the love of the truth has already been made: the oppressors of the congregation have already rejected the gospel.

God's causality reappears in **2.11–12**: 'And therefore God sends them a power that works delusion, so that they believe what is false, in order that all may be judged who did not believe the truth but had pleasure in sinfulness'. Because of their refusal to accept the love of the truth, God will punish them by making them believe in falsehood, that is, in all the cunning schemes of the lawless one depicted in 2.9–10; this belief will, in turn, lead to their condemnation (on account of the context, 'to judge' should mean here 'to condemn'). Unbelief is, so to say, punished by means of itself. The idea here is akin to that of Romans 1.18–32: God punishes the refusal of humans to acknowledge him by delivering them to sin. 2 Thessalonians 2.11–12 goes further in that the refusal itself is caused by God; this thought has its antecedents in Old Testament passages in which God is supposed to inspire false prophets (1 Kings 22.23; Ezek. 14.9), and has parallels in New Testament texts in which unbelief is seen as caused by God (e.g., John 12.39–40; Rom. 9.18, 22). We must, however, bear in mind that in the preceding verse, human responsibility was explicitly included. Apparently, the 'double causality' offered to our author (and to many others) the opportunity to reconcile the idea of God's omnipotence with the experience of refusal of the gospel and persecution of believers.

'Delusion' or 'leading astray' (*planē* in Greek), which brings about belief in 'what is false', belongs, as we saw, to the dangers of the last days. 'What is false' appears now as the opposite of 'the truth' of 2.10. In 2.12, 'believing the truth' is opposed to 'having pleasure in sinfulness'; the opposition suggests that faith has an emotional aspect. A belief that is wrong in the eyes of our author goes, in his view, hand in hand with moral depravity. In early Judaism and in early Christianity, apostasy from the one God and his envoys is thought to imply immediately apostasy from the Torah or from its Christian variant, the Law of Christ. One could here refer once more to Paul's words in Romans 1.18–32, where we also meet the opposition of 'truth' and 'sinfulness' (1.18; the same in 2.8; cf. 1 Cor. 13.6). In Matthew's version of the 'synoptic apocalypse', an increase of lawlessness is said to follow the appearance and the delusion of the false prophets (Matt. 24.11–12). In *1 Enoch* 99.8–10, the final fate of the sinners is contrasted with that of the righteous:

> They [the sinners] shall become wicked on account of the folly of their hearts; their eyes will be blindfolded on account of the fear of their hearts, the visions of their dreams. They shall become wicked and fearful through them, for they wrought all their deeds in falsehood and worshipped stone; so they shall perish instantly. In those days, blessed are they all who accept the words of wisdom and understand them, to follow the path of the Most High; they shall walk in the path of his righteousness and not become wicked with the wicked; and they shall be saved.
>
> (trans. E. Isaac, in Charlesworth 1983: 80)

In this passage, idolatry and immorality go hand in hand, and lead to perdition; belief in the one God and righteousness also go hand in hand, and lead to salvation. Similarly for the author of 2 Thessalonians: rejection of the gospel is accompanied by sinfulness, and these lead to condemnation in God's judgment. The positive contrast follows in the ensuing verses, to which we now turn.

2.13–17: THANKSGIVING, EXHORTATION AND PRAYER

The author of our letter follows up the passage on the activities of the lawless one and their effects with a second thanksgiving in **2.13–14** (cf. 1 Thess. 2.13, where we also find a second thanksgiving): 'But we are bound to thank God always for you, brothers and sisters, beloved by the Lord, because God chose you from the beginning to find salvation in sanctification by the Spirit and belief in the truth. To this end he called you through our gospel, so that you may obtain the glory of our Lord Jesus Christ'.

I recall and add to what I said on the function of this thanksgiving when analysing the structure of 2 Thessalonians (see p. 72). The thanksgiving opposes the salvation of the addressees to the doom of the unbelievers; the conjunction 'but' at its beginning serves this purpose. The topics mentioned in 2.1, Christ's coming and his gathering of the faithful, are resumed in the 'salvation' and the obtaining of 'the glory of our Lord Jesus Christ'. The second thanksgiving recalls the first thanksgiving (1.3–12): the beginning of 2.13 resembles that of 1.3; there are common themes (God's calling, 1.11; 2.14; the gospel 1.8; 2.14; the acquiring of glory 1.10, 12; 2.14). There is also a common general line of thought in the two thanksgivings: 'Paul' thanks God because of the Christian life of the congregation in view of Christ's coming. However, in the second thanksgiving the emphasis is much more on God's work in the community; it is the work God has done in them that gives 'Paul' the confidence that they will be saved. Precisely this aspect of their salvation explains why the literary form of the thanksgiving is used here. The thanksgiving as a whole serves to emphasize the importance of the preceding eschatological teaching.

After the clause in which 'Paul' expresses the obligation to give thanks – which is all but identical to the beginning of 1.3 (there are in Greek only a few minor differences) – the community is addressed as 'brothers and sisters, beloved by the Lord', a phrasing derived from 1 Thessalonians 1.4, with the significant change of 'God' into 'the Lord'. 'The Lord' refers here to Christ: that is the normal usage of our author, who has a clear interest in Jesus as 'the Lord', and 'God' is explicitly mentioned in what immediately precedes and follows. Shortly afterwards, in 2.16, God will be called the one 'who loved us'. Such an apparent lack of consistency is only to be expected for an author in the Pauline tradition. In Romans 5.5–8, God's love is said to have been shown in

the death of Christ, but according to 2 Corinthians 5.14–15 and
Galatians 2.20, Christ has shown his love in dying for the believers.
In Romans 8.35–9, Paul shifts from 'the love of Christ' (8.35) to
'the love of God' (8.39), but he adds to the latter 'that is in Jesus
Christ our Lord'. For Paul, God's love realizes itself in the love of
Christ, and the crystallization point of both is Jesus' death on the
cross. Therefore the author of 2 Thessalonians can change 'God'
from 1 Thessalonians 1.4 into 'the Lord', and ascribe the same love
to God and Jesus.

The addressees can be called 'beloved of the Lord', because God
'chose' them 'from the beginning'. The theme of God's election of
the congregation from eternity is also found elsewhere in Paul and
in the Pauline tradition (see esp. Rom. 8.28–30; Eph. 1.4–5). It has
Old Testament roots in God's election of Israel (see, e.g., Deut.
7.6–8), that is called 'beloved of him [God]' (Bar. 3.37). The goal of
God's election is 'salvation' (sōtēria in Greek), a comprehensive
indication of the bliss of the coming age, which is, in Paul's view,
already a reality in the present condition of faith (see, e.g., 2 Cor.
6.2). It may be that for our author salvation is also a present reality,
but it is evident that his main interest is in future salvation (2.10).

The salvation, for which God has chosen the congregation, is
realized 'in sanctification by the Spirit and belief in the truth'. In a
very literal translation, it says here: 'in sanctification of the spirit
and belief of the truth'. It is evident that, after 2.12, 'the truth' is the
object of 'belief', so that we can translate 'belief in the truth'. One
could be tempted to understand the other expression, 'in sanctification of the spirit' (cf. 1 Pet. 1.2), in the same way, so that
'the spirit' is the object of 'sanctification'; the result is a perfect
parallelism in the final words of 2.13. 'The spirit' has to be written
then with a lower-case letter, because it indicates the human spirit.
In my translation, 'the Spirit', with an upper-case letter, indicates
God's Spirit, who is considered as the subject of the sanctification;
hence the translation 'in sanctification by the Spirit'. In theory,
both translations are possible: the Greek word pneuma can have
both meanings (as in 1 Thess. 5.19, 23). My translation does not
yield a perfect parallelism, but it is supported by other considerations. The expression in question has been inspired, as we
saw, by 1 Thessalonians 4.7; in 4.7–8, God, who has called the
Thessalonian congregation to sanctification, is said to 'give his
Holy Spirit to you'. It is obvious that here God's Spirit is meant,
and that is then probably also the case in 2 Thessalonians 2.13. If in

2 Thessalonians 2.13 *pneuma* refers to the human spirit, the
sequence is curious: Christian life normally starts with faith and is
gradually worked out in 'sanctification of the spirit', but in our text
we would have the reverse order. However, if *pneuma* is God's Spirit,
we have a sequence that has a certain logic and is adapted to the
context: God's sanctifying work by the Spirit has precedence over
the human activity of belief in the gospel (cf. Best 1972: 315). 'To
sanctify' means 'to bring into the domain of God'. Those who
belong to God have to be holy because God is holy: 'You shall be
holy, for I am holy' (Lev. 11.44, quoted in 1 Pet. 1.16).

The words 'to this end' at the beginning of 2.14 refer to 'to find
salvation in sanctification by the Spirit and belief in the truth'. It is
to that end that God 'called you through our gospel'. God's calling
was already discussed in the comments on 1.11 (see pp. 92–3); it is
the realization in history of God's decree of election 'from the
beginning', through the preaching, by 'Paul' and his companions,
of the good news about Christ (cf. Rom. 8.30). The language used
here in our letter is redolent of predestination; however, it serves
the goal of convincing the addressees that it is indeed the eternal
God who is active in the preaching and the accepting of the gospel,
and it does not exclude human responsibility and human effort.

The final words of 2.14, 'so that you may obtain the glory of our
Lord Jesus Christ', are in apposition to the words 'to this end'.
They clarify how our author sees the contents of the general term
'salvation' (he replaces 'salvation' from 1 Thess. 5.9 by 'glory'). He
returns to a theme already discussed earlier in the letter: the
glorification of the believers (see 1.9–10, 12, and the commentary
on those verses). They will participate in the heavenly splendour
God has given to Christ. According to 1 Thessalonians 2.12, God
called the Thessalonian congregation 'to his kingdom and glory';
our author changes the goal of God's calling into 'the glory of our
Lord Jesus Christ' – which is for him hardly a change. The idea of
the participation of the believers in the glory of Christ is often
found in Paul's genuine letters (see Rom. 8.17, 29–30; 2 Cor. 3.18;
Phil. 3.21).

In **2.15**, 'Paul' explicitly resumes contact with the addressees
and draws his conclusion from the thanksgiving for God's election
of them: 'So then, brothers and sisters, stand firm and hold fast to
the traditions which you have been taught by us, either by our
word or by our letter'. The indicative of what God did in their
favour leads to the imperative of what they have to do; inversely, if

they hold fast to the teaching of 'Paul', they will be saved in the end. They are exhorted first to 'stand firm' (here used without a modifier, differently from 1 Thess. 3.8; cf. Gal. 5.1), and then to 'hold fast to the traditions'. The concept of 'tradition' (*paradosis* in Greek, from the verb *paradidonai*, 'to transmit', 'to hand down') has, in the Pauline and Deuteropauline letters, a Jewish background, as is evident from Galatians 1.14 (cf. Mark 7.1–13 and parallel). In the tractate *Aboth* ('The Fathers') from the *Mishnah* (lit. 'teaching', the codification of the oral Torah dating from *c.* 200 CE), we find the following characteristic passage: 'Moses received the Torah from Sinai and transmitted it to Joshua, and Joshua to the Elders, and the Elders to the Prophets, and the Prophets transmitted it to the men of the Great Synagogue' (1.1). In the sequel to this passage, the chain of tradition appears to go on also after 'the men of the Great Synagogue'. Both Judaism and Christianity are, as religions based on revelation of God in human history, religions of tradition. Paul speaks of various kinds of tradition: the central message of Christ's death and resurrection (1 Cor. 15.1–5), the Christian message (1 Thess. 2.13), Jesus' acts and words at the Last Supper (1 Cor. 11.23–5), practical regulations for the life of the Christian community (1 Cor. 11.2–16; 1 Thess. 4.1–8). In our Deuteropauline passage 2 Thessalonians 2.15, the 'traditions' concern primarily the preceding eschatological teaching. In 3.6, we shall meet a tradition that concerns practical regulations.

By qualifying the eschatological teaching as material handed down to 'Paul', and by him to the addressees, 'Paul' suggests that this teaching is not his own invention, but was there already before him. He only taught it to them, 'either by our word or by our letter'. As we saw in the chapter on the authorship of 2 Thessalonians, 'our word' refers, within the framework of pseudonymous fiction, to Paul's teaching when he founded the Thessalonian church (cf. 1 Thess. 1.5–2.16), and 'our letter' refers to 1 Thessalonians, and then of course especially to its eschatological parts (4.13–5.11). In 1 Thessalonians 4.15, Paul appeals for his eschatological teaching of 4.15–17 to 'a word of the Lord'; that may explain why it is called 'tradition' in 2 Thessalonians 2.15: it ultimately derives from Christ himself. 'Paul' here retrieves 1 Thessalonians from his opponents, who interpreted the letter in a wrong way (see 2.2 and the above comment on this verse). He suggests that there is no tension between the eschatological teaching of 2 Thessalonians and what Paul earlier said or wrote to the Thessalonians on the topic of eschatology. 'Paul' brings the true, reliable, traditional Pauline teaching about the end, and therefore there is no need for the addressees to lose their senses and to be alarmed (2.2); instead, they should stand firm and hold fast to the traditions they know.

In **2.16–17**, a prayer follows: 'May our Lord Jesus Christ himself and God our Father, who loved us and gave eternal comfort and good hope in grace, comfort your hearts and strengthen them in every good work and word'. The content of the exhortation in 2.15 is now put in the literary form of a prayer: may God achieve that to which the addressees are incited. 'Our Lord Jesus Christ' is mentioned first, before 'God our Father' (cf. 2 Cor. 13.13; Gal. 1.1); this order fits in well with the christological interest of our author in general, and with the important eschatological role he has ascribed to Jesus in particular (the 'normal' sequence is found in the prayer 1 Thessalonians 3.11). The words 'God our Father' are followed by 'who loved us and gave eternal comfort and good hope in grace'. In Greek this clause is construed with two singular participles; from a grammatical point of view, it has therefore to be connected with 'God our Father'. The verb of the main clause, 'may...comfort', is in the Greek text also in the singular; nevertheless, it has obviously to be connected to both subjects, Jesus and God.

Our author, who places himself in the Pauline tradition, sees the love of God, of which he speaks in 2.16, realized in the love of Jesus, which culminates in his death on the cross (see the commentary on 2.13 above). The verbal tense used in Greek (the aorist) suggests that the specific, past event of Jesus' cross, is in view.

The same tense is used when God is characterized as one who 'gave eternal comfort and good hope in grace'; most probably, we have to think here of Jesus' death and resurrection as the basis of Christian expectation. In these events and in the promise they imply, God has given comfort and hope, and thereby shown his grace. In point of fact, when speaking of 'eternal comfort and good hope', our author probably thinks also of the preceding eschatological teaching: in his message of the expected victory of Christ, the comfort and hope become tangible. 'Comfort' (*paraklēsis* in Greek, from the verb *parakalein*, used in 2.17) given by God to the oppressed community, makes it possible for them to endure the present distress. God encourages and enables them to wait for him to realize his final salvation. God's comfort is 'eternal' because it 'lasts through the judgment into the age to come' (Wanamaker 1990: 271). Beside 'comfort', 'hope' here indicates the trust that God will realize his salvation, which is still invisible but will soon become visible (cf. Rom. 8.24–5). It is called 'good' because it comes from God, who will do what he has promised. The significance for Paul of comfort and hope (based on God's act in Christ), in a situation of oppression, becomes visible in an impressive way in the blessing of 2 Corinthians 1.3–11; in 1 Thessalonians, Paul tells the Thessalonians to 'comfort one another' with the expectation of the near coming of the Lord (4.18; 5.11), an expectation that is based on Jesus' death and resurrection, and not shared by those 'who do not have hope' (4.13–14; 5.9–10). 'Hope' (*elpis* in Greek) is for Paul intimately connected with faith; it is exemplified by Abraham (see the commentary on 1.4). It seems that our author follows these lines of thought.

'Paul' prays that Christ and God 'may comfort your hearts and strengthen them in every good work and word'. Christ and God are asked to continue the comfort already given in the past, in line with the Old Testament characterization of God as the comforter of Israel and of his Anointed One as the comforter of all who mourn (see, e.g., Is. 51.12; 61.2), and also to 'strengthen' their hearts, to confirm them. The object of comforting and strengthening is 'your hearts'; the heart is the core of the human personality, and here, as often, it indicates the entire person (cf. 3.3: 'the Lord...who will strengthen *you*'). Our author combines the prayer of 1 Thessalonians 3.11–13, where we also hear of 'strengthening your hearts', with 1 Thessalonians 3.2, where we meet the same two verbs as in 2 Thessalonians 2.17 but in reverse order (although *parakalein* has there the meaning 'to exhort'). The inversion of the sequence in 2 Thessalonians 2.17 has the effect that 'to comfort' immediately follows the words on God's gift of 'eternal comfort and good hope', and that God's inward action of comforting is now followed by its outward effect of strengthening them 'in every good work and word', that is, in their entire Christian life. The final words of 2.17 announce the hortatory section that follows (cf. 3.3, 5).

Chapter 7

2 Thessalonians 3: Exhortation and letter-closing – the disorderly brothers and sisters

3.1–5: EXHORTATIONS AND PRAYER

The opening section of the third and final part of 2 Thessalonians is made up of loosely connected sentences. Still, there is a certain logic in the passage, as we saw above when we analysed the letter's structure, and as will be explained further below. 'Paul' here reinforces his bonds with the addressees, not only by using again the vocative 'brothers and sisters', but also and especially by asking them to pray for him and his companions and by praising their faith (3.1; he prayed for them in what immediately preceded); by presenting himself and his companions as their fellow sufferers from persecution (3.2, cf. 1.4); by expressing his trust that they are already doing as he says (3.4). Because of the support of the Lord (3.3, 5) and of the author's admonitions (3.4), the addressees will be kept on the right track. Thus 'Paul' makes them receptive to his specific injunctions that will follow in 3.6–12.

'Paul' starts the passage with the words: 'Finally, pray, brothers and sisters, for us' (**3.1**) This request has been derived from 1 Thessalonians 5.25; the wording of the two appeals is only slightly different. Similar requests towards the end of a letter are found in Romans 15.30, Ephesians 6.19, and Colossians 4.3 (cf. Heb. 13.18); they emphasize the reciprocity between sender and addressees. The word 'finally' comes from 1 Thessalonians 4.1; it now serves to introduce the final part of the letter (cf. 2 Cor. 13.11; Gal. 6.17; Eph. 6.10; Phil. 4.8).

Unlike 1 Thessalonians 5.25, the content of the prayer is given in two clauses. The first of these reads: 'that the word of the Lord may have a swift course and may be glorified'. 'Paul' asks them to pray for him in his role of apostle, as one sent to preach 'the word of the Lord'; that is the word about Christ in which at the same time Christ himself speaks, in other words the Christian message or the gospel (cf. 1.8; 2.14). The expression 'the word of the Lord' is found frequently in Acts (e.g., 8.25; 15.35–6); in the Pauline and Deuteropauline letters it occurs only here and in 1 Thessalonians 1.8, the probable source of our text. The imagery that the word 'may have a swift course', seems at first sight to be the well-known Pauline metaphor of the runner at the stadium, used most forcefully in 1 Corinthians 9.24–7 and also in Romans 9.16, Galatians 2.2 and 5.7, and Philippians 2.16. However, in these passages the runner is Paul or the Christian, whereas in 2 Thessalonians 3.1 it is the word. It is therefore better to see in our text an allusion to Psalm 147.15, where it is said that 'his [God's] word runs swiftly' (the LXX has here the same verb as used in 2 Thess. 3.1). Once more, an Old Testament text that concerns God is implicitly applied to Christ. It is also said that the word of the Lord 'may be glorified', that is, may be given honour because it is accepted by the believers, as in Acts 13.48; we have here a reflection of the thought of 2 Thessalonians 1.12.

In the final words of 3.1, 'as among you', the author signals once more the faith of the addressees, after his earlier remarks in 1.3–4, 10, 11; 2.13. It is not quite clear whether he refers to the moment they accepted the gospel, or to their present faith, or to both; considering the earlier remarks, it is best to suppose that both past and present are in view.

In **3.2**, the requested prayer is further said to be 'that we may be rescued from wicked and evil people'. The two clauses that give the content of the prayer clearly have to be read in connection with each other: the deliverance of 'Paul' and his companions concerns them in their role as preachers of 'the word of the Lord'. In Romans 15.30–1 and 2 Corinthians 1.8–11, we find in more extensive form references to external threats to Paul and his fellow workers and to the congregation's prayer for them. Opposition to, and persecution of, 'Paul' are especially prominent in 2 Timothy (a Deuteropauline letter; see 3.10–11; 4.16–18). Apparently, these elements become an important part of the image of Paul in the time after his death, as is also evident from Acts, where opposition and persecution are almost standard elements in the reactions to Paul's proclamation of the gospel (see, e.g., 13.45, 50; 14.5, and 17.5–9, on Paul's visit to Thessalonica). Paul suffers the same fate as his Master, Jesus. Just as the description of Jesus' fate has been influenced by Old Testament texts on the sufferings of the righteous one (such as Psalms 22 and 69; see, e.g., Mark 15.22–37), so Paul's fate is depicted in similar terms (cf. 2 Thess. 3.2 with Ps. 140.1, or 2 Tim. 4.17 with Ps. 22.22).

The existence of 'wicked and evil people' is explained at the end of 3.2: 'for faith is not everyone's business'. It is simply observed that not all have accepted the gospel. Indirectly, unbelievers are qualified as 'wicked and evil people'. We meet here the clear distinction between 'we' and 'they', between good and bad, which, as we saw in the chapter on the milieu of 2 Thessalonians, is characteristic of apocalyptic eschatology. We encounter the language of a small, oppressed minority trying to maintain its hope, its identity and its coherence in a hostile world; such language should not be abused in other situations or contexts.

In **3.3**, a formulaic sentence follows: 'But the Lord is faithful, he who will strengthen you and guard you from the evil one' (cf. 1 Cor. 1.9; 10.13; 1 Thess. 5.24). Between this verse and the preceding one, there is a connection by catchword: in the Greek text, 3.2 ends with 'faith' (*pistis*), and 3.3. begins with 'faithful' (*pistos*). There is also an opposition between the unbelievers of 3.2 and the faithful addressed in 3.3. Finally, there is a link between the evil people of 3.2, who threaten Paul, and 'the evil one' of 3.3, who will not get hold on the congregation; in the light of 2.9, we may suppose that 'the evil one' is behind the evil people. The Christian community, with Jesus as the Lord who directs their lives, is fenced off from the unbelievers, who are governed by 'the evil one'.

The saying of 3.3 has probably been inspired by 1 Thessalonians 5.24: 'He who calls you [God] is faithful, he who will also do it'. Significantly, God is again replaced by Christ: Christ is now the one who can be trusted. The Lord will strengthen the community, an activity that was prayed for in 2.17. He will also 'guard you from the evil one', as in the Old Testament God is said to 'guard' Israel and its individual members (see, e.g., Exod. 23.20; Ps. 17.8; esp. Psalm 121). The words translated by 'from the evil one' can also be translated by 'from evil'. The former translation has to be preferred on account of the mention of Satan in 2.9; he is also mentioned twice in 1 Thessalonians, used by our author (2.18; 3.5: 'the tempter').

In the next verse (**3.4**), we switch again from divine to human activity, a switch that we observed elsewhere in 2 Thessalonians (1.11; 2.10–17), and that will also occur between 3.4 and 5. The author now testifies to his trust that the addressees follow and will follow his instructions: 'In the Lord we have confidence in you, that you are doing and will continue to do what we command'. We have here another connection by catchword, but weaker than the former one: 'I have confidence' is in Greek *pepoitha*, from the same root *peith-* that is also at the basis of *pistis* and *pistos*. The words of 3.4 are the human reverse of the saying of the preceding verse: if the Lord indeed strengthens and guards the addressees, Paul can have confidence that they will do what he orders.

Against the background of 3.3, it is fitting that 'Paul' locates his confidence 'in the Lord'. The expressions 'in Christ', 'in the Lord', and the like, occur frequently in Paul's genuine letters, and characterize the relationship between Christ and the Christians: they 'are in Christ' (2 Cor. 5.17), they are 'living for God in Jesus Christ' (Rom. 6.11), they 'stand firm in the Lord' (1 Thess. 3.8). The expression basically has a spatial meaning, indicating that the Christians are within the sphere of Christ's power (cf. 1.1), but various nuances are possible in the preposition 'in', so that 'in the Lord' and the like sometimes simply means 'Christian' (e.g., in Rom. 16.11). In our case, the author has his confidence in the addressees 'in the Lord': he knows that it is the Lord who works in them and in him. As a consequence, he can rely that they are already doing and will do in the future what he commands. The verb 'to command' (*paraggellein* in Greek) has a connotation of authority. Its occurrence here has probably been inspired by 1 Thessalonians 4.2, and the juxtaposition of the addressees' present and future doing may come from 1 Thessalonians 4.1.

It is evident that 2 Thessalonians 3.4 especially prepares for and announces what follows in 3.6–12: the latter passage deals with a specific problem in the practical behaviour of part of the congregation, and in 3.6, 10, 12 the verb 'to command' is again used when the author brings forward his past and present answer to the problem. Before that, however, he inserts a prayer; again the Lord is invoked, this time to make the congregation concentrate on the right aim: 'May the Lord direct your hearts towards the love of God and the steadfast expectation of Christ' (**3.5**). It seems that the prayer of 1 Thessalonians 3.11–13 has been the example for the first half of the verse: 'May the Lord direct' comes from 1 Thessalonians 3.11; it is now combined with the object 'your hearts' that is found in 1 Thessalonians 3.13. 'Our God and Father' as the first subject has been omitted in 2 Thessalonians; instead, the

author of our letter has apparently been led by 1 Thessalonians
3.12, where 'the Lord' alone is the subject of the second part of
the prayer. The resultant expression 'to direct the heart' is used
in the Old Testament for the concentration of human attention
on God (see esp. 1 Chron. 29.18, in a prayer of King David:
'direct their [the people's] hearts towards you'; also, e.g., 2
Chron. 12.14; Sir. 49.3).

Here, the goal towards which the hearts have to be directed is
'the love of God and the steadfast expectation of Christ'. The
words 'of God' are either a subjective or an objective genitive: the
text concerns either God's love for the congregation, or their love
for God. It is hard to tell which one of the two possibilities the
author has in view. In the Greek behind the words translated as
'the steadfast expectation of Christ', there is a similar ambiguity.
Connected with the Greek word *hupomonē*, 'steadfastness', the
words 'of Christ' can be a subjective genitive, and in that case we
should translate 'the steadfastness of Christ', that is, the steadfastness Christ himself has. It can also be an objective genitive,
and then we are dealing here with the steadfastness of which Christ
is the object; hence the translation: 'the steadfast expectation
of Christ'. I have adopted the latter translation because in 1.4
'steadfastness' obviously indicates a virtue of the addressees. We
may surmise the same to be the case in 3.5: the congregation is
the subject of the steadfastness, and Christ has then to be its
object. This interpretation concurs with the interest of the author
of 2 Thessalonians in Christ's parousia, and with the exhortative
character of 2 Thessalonians 3. It also suggests that 'the love of
God' means 'the love you have for God' – although the imperfect
parallelism of the genitival constructions at the end of 2.13 makes
it possible that we have in 3.5 a comparable imperfect parallelism.

3.6: THE INJUNCTION TO HOLD ALOOF FROM THE
DISORDERLY BROTHERS AND SISTERS

The preceding general exhortation is now followed by a specific
one: 'We command you, brothers and sisters, in the name of our
Lord Jesus Christ, that you hold aloof from any brother or sister
who lives in a disorderly way and not in accord with the tradition
they received from us' (**3.6**). 'Paul' commands the community
'in the name of our Lord Jesus Christ': the Lord is invoked to
enhance the authority with which the command is given. It is

not just 'Paul' who commands, but actually it is the Lord. The command (apparently influenced by 1 Thess. 4.1 and 5.14; cf. 1 Cor. 5.9–11) implies that the members of the congregation should hold aloof from members who display a certain kind of behaviour: they live 'in a disorderly way and not in accord with the tradition they received from us'. What does this qualification of their way of living (see also 3.7, 11) mean?

As it seems, their behaviour amounts to a refusal to work for a living. However, the Greek word translated with 'disorderly' (*ataktos*), does not in itself denote, as C. Spicq has demonstrated with ample evidence (Spicq 1956), laziness or work-shyness, but only that the person(s) or thing(s) indicated resist some kind of order. What order is exactly meant, depends upon the context in which the word is used. In 2 Thessalonians, the context provides sufficient clues to determine what kind of order is meant. First of all, in 3.6 'living in a disorderly way' is paralleled with 'not living in accord with the tradition they received from us'. In 3.7–8, the fact that 'Paul' was not disorderly among the addressees of the letter is paralleled with the fact that he did not eat anyone's bread without paying; in contrast he worked day and night, in toil and hardship, so as not to be a burden to anyone from the congregation. In 3.11–12, finally, 'living in a disorderly way' is explained as 'not doing any work but being busybodies', and people who do so are admonished 'to eat their own bread, doing work in quietness'. Of importance is also the maxim of 3.10, to which 'Paul' refers as his earlier oral instruction to them: 'if anyone will not work, let him or her not eat either'. This maxim here suggests that the 'disorderly ones' were not willing to work.

So, the order which is at stake in 2 Thessalonians 3.6–12 is part of the tradition which the addressees received, and it implies that one should work for his own living (cf. 1 Thess. 4.11), instead of taking advantage of others. To determine this 'order' in a more specific way, we should consider, first of all, that in early Christian usage the substantive 'tradition', as well as the verbs 'to transmit', and 'to receive (from tradition)', often concern rules of conduct for the life of the Christian community (as is evidently the case in 2 Thess. 3.6) which derive, via Jewish tradition, from the Old Testament. The ethical tradition transmitted by Paul in 1 Thessalonians 4.1–8 has an Old Testament and Jewish colour, and the transmitted rules of conduct of 1 Corinthians 11.2–16 are largely determined by Genesis 1–3. In 2 Peter 2.21, 'the holy commandment transmitted to them [the false teachers]' is paralleled with 'the way of righteousness'.

A second consideration also directs us towards an Old Testament provenance of the 'order' which is the matter at issue in 2 Thessalonians 3.6–12. The Greek verb *tassein*, 'to order' (from which *ataktos*, 'disorderly', derives), and its derivatives are used in early Jewish and early Christian literature to indicate the order which is ordered in the Law by God or by Moses (this is the case in the LXX version of Lev. 18.4 and Deut. 27.1; in Philo's *On the Special Laws* 2.175, where he writes: 'The law orders'; in Mark 1.44 and parallels, in Acts 7.44, to mention just a few examples). The order instituted by God at the creation is indicated in the same way (e.g., in the LXX version of Job 38.12; in Wis. 11.20 and Acts 17.26).

The above means that it seems worthwhile to look for an Old Testament 'order' which could be at the base of what 'Paul' tries to inculcate in 2 Thessalonians 3.6–12. Such a thing is easily found in Genesis 3.17–19, God's words to Adam after the Fall:

...cursed is the earth because of you;
in pain you shall eat of it
all the days of your life.
Thorns and thistles it will produce for you;
and you shall eat the plants of the field.
In the sweat of your face you shall eat bread....

It is evident that in this passage God institutes an order to which human beings are subject: they have to work hard for their living. Josephus in his *Jewish Antiquities* 1.51 refers to God's words in Genesis 3.14–19 by saying that 'God ordered them to suffer these things'. Also elsewhere in early Jewish literature, the fact that humans have to work hard for their living is considered to be an order established by God after the Fall. Sirach 7.15 speaks of 'toilsome labour and agriculture, created by the most High'. In *Sibylline Oracles* 1.57–8 (a Jewish text probably dating from around the turn of the era), God says to the first humans after the Fall: 'Increase, multiply, and work on earth with skill, so that by sweat you may have your fill of food' (trans. J. J. Collins, in Charlesworth 1983: 336).

I resume: the reproach, in 2 Thessalonians 3.6, of living without order and not according to the tradition may very well be understood as a reproach of not accepting an order imposed by God in the Old Testament. More specifically, it may very well concern Genesis 3.17–19, a passage understood in Jewish tradition as God's imposition upon man of the obligation to work hard in order to be able to eat. What remains to be demonstrated, is that there are some literary connections between 2 Thessalonians 3.6–12 and Genesis 3.17–19 as understood around the beginning of our era, which make it probable that the passage from 2 Thessalonians indeed alludes to this Old Testament passage.

First of all, in 2 Thessalonians 3.6–12 the same central terms and ideas are used that are present in the passage from Genesis. 'Paul' says in 3.8 that 'we did not eat any one's bread for nothing, but we worked in toil and hardship', and accordingly, the disorderly brothers are admonished in 3.12 'to eat their own bread, doing work in quietness', in agreement with the maxim of 3.10: 'if anyone will not work, let him or her not eat either'. In Genesis 3.17–19, we meet: '...cursed is the earth because of you; in pain you shall eat of it...and you shall eat the plants of the field. In the sweat of your face you shall eat your bread'. Both content and terminology ('to eat [bread]', 'to work') of Genesis 3.17–19 and of 2 Thessalonians 3.6–12 are similar.

Secondly, we may observe that in several later versions of Genesis 3.17–19 (which at least in part are certainly pre-Christian or contemporaneous with the beginnings of Christianity) it is stressed even more than it was already in the Hebrew text that working is the condition for eating, just as in 2 Thessalonians 3.7–8, 10, 12. In the LXX version of Genesis 3.17, the words 'cursed is the earth because of you' from the Hebrew text have become 'cursed is the earth in your works' (in Hebrew, there is a difference of one letter between 'because of you' and 'in your works'; the Greek translator read the latter instead of the former). The effect of this translation, when it is read together with the following verse 3.19, is that now work itself participates in the curse: only by hard and toilsome work will man be able to eat, to provide for his living. The Palestinian Targums (a Targum is a paraphrase of the Hebrew Old Testament in Aramaic) have after Genesis 3.18 an addition compared with the Hebrew text, in which Adam is made to say, among other things: 'So let us rise and work with the work of our hands and we shall eat food from the food of the earth'. In one of these Targums, the *Targum Pseudo-Jonathan*, the beginning of Genesis 3.19 is rendered as follows: 'From the work of your hand you will eat food'.

From the above, we can conclude that the order at stake in 2 Thessalonians 3.6–12 is probably that of Genesis 3.17–19 (so also, e.g., Agrell 1976: 120–5). God instituted there – so the text was read in Jewish tradition – the order according to which humans have to work hard for their food. The fact that the author of 2 Thessalonians does not make the allusion to Genesis 3.17–19 explicit, cannot be an argument against the reality of the allusion: he never explicitly refers to the Old Testament, but evidently assumes his readers to be able to detect such hints.

In the topic of the disorderly brothers and sisters who refuse to work for a living, two elements found in 1 Thessalonians seem to have been combined. In 1 Thessalonians 4.11–12, Paul exhorts the Thessalonian congregation 'to work with your own hands, as we commanded you, so that you may live decently towards the outsiders, and be dependent upon nobody', and later, in 1 Thessalonians 5.14, the members of the church are urged 'to admonish the disorderly ones'. These rather general admonitions from 1 Thessalonians on work and on disorderliness recur in the second letter in a much more specific way and with different motives (cf. 1 Thess. 4.12 with 2 Thess. 3.7–10). It should be noted that within 1 Thessalonians, there is no direct relation between the two passages, and it remains unclear what order is violated by the disorderly ones mentioned in 5.14. The author of 2 Thessalonians combines the two passages: for him, the disorderly ones are those who refuse to work with their own hands.

Our author apparently addresses a new problem with the help of what he found here and there in 1 Thessalonians. It is striking that in his argument in 3.6–12, he does not revert to the first letter, but – fictitiously, of course – to Paul's founding visit to the community. That may confirm that we have here a problem that differs indeed from the problems dealt with in 1 Thessalonians (cf. Laub 1973: 146, 151).

3.7–10: THE EXAMPLE OF 'PAUL'

After these necessary elaborations on the order violated by the disorderly ones and on the relation of 2 Thessalonians 3.6–12 with 1 Thessalonians, 3.7–10 can be discussed rather briefly. The conjunction 'for' at the beginning of 3.7 shows that 'Paul' now advances his arguments to buttress the command of 3.6. The arguments concern his stay, in the past, with the community: then, as they know, he demonstrated both by his own behaviour (3.7–9) and by his words (3.10) that one has to work for a living.

He starts by telling his addressees that they themselves 'know how one ought to imitate us' (**3.7a**). Both the reference to their own knowledge and the theme of 'imitation' come from 1 Thessalonians (see 1 Thess. 2.1; 3.3; 5.2, and 1.6; 2.14). The related themes of the 'imitation of Paul' and of 'Paul as an example', also found in 2 Thessalonians 3.9, occur a few times in Paul's genuine letters. A congregation has to imitate Paul, who is an example for them (1 Cor. 4.16; 11.1; Phil. 3.17; 1 Thess. 1.6). Imitating Paul implies imitating Christ, because Paul imitates Christ (1 Cor. 11.1; 1 Thess. 1.6). Congregations can also be an example worth imitating for each other (1 Thess. 1.7; 2.14). In the (Deuteropauline) Pastorals, the addressees, Timothy and Titus, are admonished to be an example for the believers (1 Tim. 4.12; Tit. 2.7). In 2 Thessalonians, the idea is applied in a peculiar way. It concerns one quite specific aspect of the behaviour of 'Paul': the fact that he did not live at the expense of others, but that he supported himself. Moreover, the example of 'Paul' has become part of the tradition mentioned in 3.6. His 'apostolic behaviour' has become a detailed standard for future generations of believers.

The conduct of 'Paul' is then explained, first negatively: 'for we did not live among you in a disorderly way, and we did not eat any one's bread for nothing' (**3.7b-8**). 'Paul' respected the order of Genesis 3.17–19, that one should eat bread in the sweat of one's face. He here employs the Old Testament expression 'to eat bread', tantamount to 'to feed oneself' (in addition to Gen. 3.19, see, e.g., 2 Kings 4.8). He did not sponge on others.

Next, he opposes a positive description of his behaviour: 'but we worked in toil and hardship, night and day, so as not to be a burden to any one of you'. A single reference to his working would in itself have been enough in opposition to sponging on others; the qualifications 'in toil and hardship, night and day' are added to enhance the seriousness of his efforts in earning his own livelihood. As already observed, the wording of 3.8b is an all but literal repetition of 1 Thessalonians 2.9. There, Paul speaks of his preaching of the gospel; the entire context (1 Thess. 2.1–12) shows that he worked very hard in order to secure himself against the suspicion that, just as certain popular philosophers or certain other Christian preachers, he preached his message in the hope of personal profit. He makes the same point in 1 Corinthians 9.12, 15–18 and 2 Corinthians 11.7–8 and 12.13. The passages from 2 Corinthians show that this was not a general line of conduct on

Paul's part; his choice apparently depended on the chance that the suspicion just mentioned could arise. In 2 Thessalonians however, the link to the preaching of the gospel is not made; we observe again that the 'apostolic behaviour' is valued in itself.

We can make the same observation concerning **3.9**: 'not that we do not have the right, but to hold up ourselves as an example for you to imitate'. As the real Paul does in 1 Corinthians 9.4, 6 (see his arguments in 9.7–14), and in very similar wording, 'Paul' insists that he has a right to be supported by the congregation. However, the motive to waive this right is different: in 1 Corinthians, it is to avoid hindrance to the propagation of the gospel (9.12), to show that his preaching is a task entrusted to him (9.15–18); but in 2 Thessalonians, it is to make himself into an example to be imitated by the congregation. We see once more that the conduct of 'Paul' is detached from the gospel and esteemed in itself.

After these references to his past conduct, 'Paul' puts forward what he said in the past as another argument in favour of the command of 3.6, and also to show that he acted in agreement with his own words: 'For even when we were with you, we used to give you this command: if anyone will not work, let him or her not eat either' (**3.10**; cf. 1 Thess. 3.4). The command has heavily influenced Christian thought on labour, especially on the labour of monks (see Trilling 1980: 148–50). Numerous parallels to the maxim adduced here by 'Paul' have been found, in the Old Testament and in Jewish and pagan literature (although no literal ones); mostly, these constitute simple truisms ('if you do not work, you have nothing to eat'). So we read in the Book of Proverbs: 'He who tills his land will be sated with bread' (12.11 = 28.19), or: 'A sluggish person will go hungry' (19.15). In the *Sentences* of Pseudo-Phocylides, a Jewish collection of wisdom sayings probably dating from the period between 30 BCE and 40 CE, we find the saying: 'Work hard so that you can live from your own means; for every idle man lives from what his hands can steal' (153–4; trans. P. W. van der Horst, in Charlesworth 1985: 579). A nice pagan parallel is found in the words of the ant to the fly in Phaedrus, *Fables*, 4.25.17 (dating from the first half of the first century CE): 'You do no work? That's why you don't have anything when you need it' (trans. B. E. Perry, in Perry 1965: 341). As a proverb, the maxim from 2 Thessalonians 3.10 is widely used, but almost always in the mutilated form: 'If you won't work you shan't eat'. In this form, it even entered the constitution of the

Soviet Union of 1936. The parallels and mutilated quotations, and also the immediate context, make it obvious that the accent in the maxim is on 'willing': those who are able to work should do so instead of taking advantage of others. In its context in 2 Thessalonians, it reminds the addressees of the fact that the order that God imposed on humanity in Genesis 3.17–19, is still valid. One should beware of taking this maxim out of its literary and historical context, and of making it, in mutilated form, into a law, saying that to have an income to live on is a right for the economically useful and a favour granted to the others. On that point, early Christians in fact thought quite differently (see, e.g., Matt. 25.31–46; Eph. 4.28).

3.11–12: THE INJUNCTION TO THE DISORDERLY BROTHERS AND SISTERS

After the digression on his exemplary conduct and word, 'Paul' returns to the topic broached in 3.6: the behaviour of the disorderly ones. He first refers to news that has reached him: 'For we hear that some are living among you in a disorderly way, not doing any work but being busybodies' (**3.11**). The fact that news reached 'Paul' (in what form, is not clear), explains why he made the preceding digression; therefore, he starts with 'for'. Some members of the congregation are, as we already saw, not accepting the order of Genesis 3.17–19; this time, this conduct is clarified as 'not doing any work but being busybodies'. In Greek, we have a play on words between *ergazomenous*, 'doing work', and *periergazomenous*, 'being busybodies'. What exactly is implied in 'being busybodies' depends on how one assesses the relationship between the eschatological error of 2.2 and the disorderly behaviour discussed in 3.6–12.

In **3.12**, the disorderly ones themselves are addressed, not directly but in the third person: 'Such people we command and exhort in the Lord Jesus Christ to eat their own bread, doing work in quietness'. It is somewhat surprising to meet 'to exhort' after 'to command', as if the severity of the command is immediately mitigated to the gentleness of the exhortation. However, the combination of the two verbs has apparently been derived from the double occurrence in 1 Thessalonians 4.1–2, 10–11. The two verbs are not quite synonymous, but certainly in the same line. The expression 'in the Lord Jesus Christ' parallels 'in the name of our Lord Jesus Christ' in 3.6. For its meaning, I refer to the commentary on 3.4. Here, it is evidently used to give the authority of the Lord himself to the command and exhortation. The disorderly ones are commanded and exhorted to earn their own livelihood; it is of course supposed that they are able to do so.

They should do their work 'in quietness'; that is, they should not 'be busybodies'. The words 'in quietness' have been inspired by 1 Thessalonians 4.11. There, the exhortation to live quietly is motivated by the esteem of the congregation in the eyes of the outsiders (4.12; cf. 1 Tim. 2.2); here, such a motive is not mentioned. In the case of 2 Thessalonians, the motive will become clear when we gain an understanding of the relationship between the eschatological error of 2.2 and the wrong conduct of 3.6–12. I now turn to that question; the answer to it is essential to an understanding of 2 Thessalonians as a whole, because the disorderly conduct of some members of the congregation and the commotion caused by the message that 'the day of the Lord has come' (2.2) constitute the only two *specific* issues in 2 Thessalonians.

It is not surprising that many commentators have thought some kind of link exists between the two: the eschatological error is supposed to be the source of the wrong conduct. It seems only logical to surmise such a causal relationship: it would be strange indeed if, in such a short letter as 2 Thessalonians, the only two specific problems discussed were not to be related. It is true that the author does not explicitly connect the two problems. That, however, is not a compelling argument against the connection: if the addressees already knew the problems were related, there was no need for the author to make the relationship explicit.

There are, moreover, some indications in the letter which at least suggest a link between the two issues. The procedures 'Paul' follows in his efforts to solve the two problems, display similarities. In both instances, he refers to what he said when he was with the congregation (2.5; 3.10), he appeals to their knowledge (2.6; 3.7), and he places the apostolic tradition, received by the congregation, in position against the apparently wrong teaching or behaviour (2.15; 3.6). The section on the disorderly ones immediately follows a reference to 'the steadfast expectation of Christ' (3.5). This sequence would also suggest some connection between eschatological expectation and (fight against) disorderly behaviour.

A sociological explanation for the disorderly behaviour, based on labour relations and social relationships between patrons and clients in the Roman Empire at the time the letter was written (see

Russell 1988; Winter 1989), may have some validity, but it only elucidates the possibility of people being unemployed or dependent for their livelihood upon others. What it leaves unclear, is the motive for their not being *willing* to work (cf. 2 Thess. 3.10c), and thereby being a burden to others (cf. 3.8). A sociological approach explains why people are without work; another explanation is required for their unwillingness to work (see for criticism of Russell also Romaniuk 1993).

In my view there is indeed, in 2 Thessalonians, a relationship between eschatological error and disorderly behaviour. Such a relationship may be considered as proved if it can be demonstrated that the specific kind of disorderly behaviour combated in 3.6–12 can be explained as caused by the specific character of the eschatological error combated in 2.1–12. So the question to be asked is not simply whether there is in general a relationship between eschatological error and disorderly conduct, but what kind of relationship there is between the two definite varieties of both as they occur in 2 Thessalonians.

We saw that the order violated by the disorderly ones is probably that of Genesis 3.17–19, where God ordained that humans have to work hard for their food. We also saw that the phrase 'the day of the Lord has come' (2 Thess. 2.2) meant for its adherents (as our author understood them) that Christ had already returned on earth and was performing his eschatological task, or was on the point of doing so. The question is then: what can this conviction that the parousia has taken place have to do with the refusal of the disorderly ones to accept the order of Genesis 3.17–19?

In early Jewish and early Christian apocalypticism as it was current at the beginning of our era, absence of hunger, thirst and labour belongs to the blessings of the new era. Or, to put it positively: those who will participate in the coming age will have plenty of food and drink, and will enjoy freedom from labour. In *Sibylline Oracles* 3.619–23 (dating from the second century BCE), for instance, we read about the time of the end:

And then God will give great joy to men,
for earth and trees and countless flocks of sheep
will give to men the true fruit
of wine, sweet honey and white milk
and corn, which is best of all for mortals.

                    (trans. J. J. Collins, in Charlesworth 1983: 376)

Christian examples can be found in Revelation 7.16 and 21.1–22.5.
This kind of expectation for the future has been inspired by
Old Testament passages such as Isaiah 49.10 and 58.11 and
Ezekiel 34.29.

Frequently it takes the form of expecting the restoration of
paradisiac conditions, or of Paradise itself, on analogy with some
prophetic passages from the Old Testament dealing with the
restoration of Zion, or of the land, so that it will be like the Garden
of Eden (Is. 51.3; Ezek. 36.35), and with the restoration of the
original good relations of animals and men (Hos. 2.20; Is. 11.6–8;
65.25). A clear example is to be found in 2 Baruch 73.1–74.1, where
the time of salvation is described in terms strongly reminiscent of
the Old Testament descriptions of Paradise and seen as the reversal
of the curses of Genesis 3.16–19:

> And it will happen that after he [the Anointed One] has brought
> down everything which is in the world, and has sat down in
> eternal peace on the throne of the kingdom, then joy will be
> revealed and rest will appear. And then health will descend
> in dew, and illness will vanish, and fear and tribulation and
> lamentation will pass away from among men, and joy will
> encompass the earth. And nobody will again die untimely, nor
> will any adversity take place suddenly....And the wild beasts will
> come from the wood and serve man, and the asps and dragons
> will come out of their holes to subject themselves to a child. And
> women will no longer have pain when they bear, nor will they be
> tormented when they yield the fruits of their womb. And it will
> happen in those days that the reapers will not become tired, and
> the farmers will not wear themselves out, because the products of
> themselves will shoot out speedily, during the time that they work
> on them in full tranquillity.
>
> (trans. A. F. J. Klijn, in Charlesworth 1983: 645–6)

In 4 Ezra 2.12, God says to Ezra about the coming age: 'The tree of
life shall give them [God's people] fragrant perfume, and they
shall neither toil nor become weary'; according to 8.52, he says to
Ezra and the other righteous: '...it is for you that Paradise is
opened, the tree of life is planted, the age to come is prepared,
plenty is provided, a city is built, rest is appointed, goodness
is established and wisdom perfected beforehand' (trans. B. M.
Metzger, in Charlesworth 1983: 527, 544). Many other passages in
the field of apocalyptic eschatology contain similar descriptions of

eschatological bliss in terms of Paradise, in which the abundance of food, often associated with the tree of life, and the absence of toil and labour are prominent themes (see, e.g., Rev. 2.7; 22.2, 14, 19). This way of interpreting final salvation apparently belonged to the usual repertory of apocalyptic eschatology, and, in view of its currency, it is quite probable that the conviction combated in 2 Thessalonians 2.2, that 'the day of the Lord' had come, implied a conception of this day in terms of, among other things, the restoration of Paradise or of paradisiac conditions.

We are now in a position to explain in a very precise way the disorderly behaviour combated in 2 Thessalonians 3.6–12 by means of the eschatological error combated in 2.1–12. The content of the eschatological error is, that the parousia of the Lord has taken place. He has returned, and is already performing his task or is on the point of doing so. This task implies defeating the satanic powers still at work (cf. 2 Thess. 2.8–10), executing judgment (cf. 1.8–9; 2.12) and bringing salvation to the believers (cf. 1.5, 7, 10; 2.13–14). In the fashion of apocalyptic eschatology, the regaining of Paradise or at least the restoration of paradisiac conditions is also part of this salvation. When Christ has returned, the restoration of Paradise and the annulment of the curse of Genesis 3.17–19 are being realized or will be very soon; therefore, there is no need to work any more, in toil and trouble, for a living. There is no longer any need to adhere to the order, imposed by God after the Fall, of having to work hard before enjoying food, because this order has been or is being annulled. And that is exactly the conduct of the disorderly ones of 2 Thessalonians 3.6–12. They do not obey the order of 3.10: 'If anyone will not work, let him not eat'. In fact of course they live at the expense of others (as suggested in 3.8, 12), because they have to eat something after all. Instead of 'doing work in quietness', they are busybodies (3.11), which may very well refer to their activities to proclaim their message of the realized parousia (2.2). Over against their message and their disorderly conduct, 'Paul' inculcates on the one hand that the parousia will not take place before certain events which have not yet occurred (2.3–12), and on the other hand that the order of Genesis 3.17–19 is still in force, as the example of his own conduct shows (3.6–12). He requires quietness instead of eschatologically motivated unrest. He tries to give his readers a sense of 'eschatological realism': as long as definite salvation has not yet been realized, they should not behave as if it already had.

They are still living in the situation of Paradise lost; it has not yet been regained.

It is, of course, impossible to prove in a definite way that the disorderly behaviour of some members of the congregation, as discussed in 2 Thessalonians 3.6–12, was caused by the realized eschatology which the author of 2 Thessalonians combats in 2.1–12. I have tried to show in the above, however, that a causal relationship between these two issues via the eschatological abolition of the order of Genesis 3.17–19 is at least a very plausible hypothesis. It has the advantage of connecting the distinctive doctrinal and ethical issues of 2 Thessalonians not in a general, but in a specific way, and it fits in with the data of the letter itself.

3.13–16: EXHORTATIONS AND PRAYER

The exhortative section of 2 Thessalonians ends as it started: with exhortations of a general kind, followed by a prayer. Many scholars are inclined to connect these verses with the preceding passage on the disorderly ones; in their view, 'our word' in 3.14 would refer to the command given in 3.12, and the order of 3.14 would be comparable to that of 3.6. To my mind, it is preferable to consider 3.13–16 as a small unit in itself within the exhortative section of the letter. It starts with the vocative 'brothers and sisters', which marks a new beginning, just as in 3.1–5 and 3.6–12, and there is no indication in the text of 3.13–16 to suggest that 'Paul' is still discussing the question of the disorderly behaviour of some members of the congregation (so also Trilling 1980: 154–5; Müller 1988: 166–8).

The first exhortation is very general: 'But you, brothers and sisters, do not tire of doing good' (**3.13**). The conjunction 'but' opposes the exhortation to the preceding injunction to the disorderly ones; now the other members are addressed, as in 3.6. General ethical teachings of this kind are common at the end of Pauline and Deuteropauline letters (see, e.g., 1 Cor. 16.13–14, and esp. Gal. 6.9, close in wording to 2 Thess. 3.13).

In **3.14**, 'Paul' gives his instruction on how to deal with disobedient members: 'If anyone does not obey our word in this letter, mark that person, and have nothing to do with them, so that they may be ashamed'. 'This letter' (lit. 'the letter') can only refer to the present letter, 2 Thessalonians. 'Our word in this letter' is then an indication of the entire content of the letter; it is self-evident that it includes his injunction to the disorderly ones in 3.12, but it encompasses more. The author clearly states that the addressees have to comply with everything he has written in the letter. The function of this information is to give the letter the status and the authority of an apostolic letter: 'the apostle Paul' is supposed to speak here, he is speaking on behalf of the Lord Jesus Christ himself, and his words have to be obeyed. Together with the prescript (1.1–2) and the injunction to hold fast to the Pauline traditions which are supposed to be found in 2 Thessalonians (2.15), the verses 3.14–15, and also 3.17, serve to make the letter into an apostolic letter.

The community is urged to mark a disobedient person. The person in question has also to be avoided: one should have no dealings with him or her. The aim of this measure is that the disobedient persons may be ashamed: the intended effect of the exclusion from the community is that the excluded will see the error of their ways. One receives the impression that the measures depicted here are less severe than what Paul tells the Corinthian congregation to do in the case of a grave sexual offence (1 Cor. 5.1–13).

This impression is strengthened by what follows in **3.15** (where elements from 1 Thessalonians 5.12–14 seem to have exerted some influence): 'And do not consider this person as an enemy, but admonish them as a brother or sister'. Members of the congregation, against whom the measures of 3.14 have been taken, do not become hostile outsiders, but they continue to be members of the community, and as such the other members should talk to them, trying to convince them to change their ways.

There is a certain tension in the measures described in 3.14–15: on the one hand, 'Paul' speaks of strict exclusion from the community; on the other hand, the exclusion has the aim of bringing about a change of attitude in the excluded person. The exclusion is obviously not a total one, but it is only temporary, and it leaves possibilities for contact. Although it is not precisely clear how we are to imagine the marking and avoiding, we might suppose for instance, that the names of the offenders were read in a liturgical assembly, and that the persons in question were excluded from it. In that case, we have both a strict, formal exclusion, and the possibility for admonishment.

Passages such as the present one are the first evidence of the development of church discipline. Other evidence is found within the New Testament in 1 Corinthians 5.1–13, already mentioned, and in Matthew 18.15–18, and Titus 3.10–11, where fairly detailed regulations are given on how to deal with offenders within the Christian community. It is only logical that a community or communities seeking an own identity should develop ways of handling what is experienced as an infringement of that identity. In rabbinic Judaism, various degrees of exclusion from the community were known; in the writings of the Qumran sect, we find regulations for the treatment of all kinds of offenders against rules that established the strict limits of the community. By way of example, I quote a few lines from the *Community Rule* which are somewhat similar to 2 Thessalonians 3.14–15 (a global accusation, and a temporary sanction implying exclusion from the liturgical assembly):

> And no man among the members of the Covenant of the Community who deliberately, on any point whatever, turns aside from all that is commanded, shall touch the pure Meal of the men of holiness or know anything of their counsel until his deeds are purified from all falsehood and he walks in perfection of way.
>
> (8.16–18; trans. G. Vermes, in Vermes 1975: 86)

A prayer for peace follows: 'May the Lord of peace himself give you peace at all times in all ways' (**3.16**). It has been modelled after the prayer to 'the God of peace' in 1 Thessalonians 5.23; a similar prayer occurs in Romans 15.33. Assurances of the assistance of 'the God of peace' are found, also towards the end of a letter, in Romans 16.20, 2 Corinthians 13.11, and Philippians 4.9. The closing of the priestly blessing of Numbers 6.24–6 constitutes an Old Testament precedent for the prayer for peace: 'May the Lord...give you peace' (6.26; cf. Is. 26.12). We observe once again that our author has replaced 'God' by 'the Lord': the prayer for peace is now directed to the exalted Christ, who bears God's name and exercises God's functions. Just as in 2 Thessalonians 1.2, 'peace' is here an inclusive indication of the eschatological salvation which Christ will finally bring at his parousia (cf. 1.6–10) and which is already working in the present; the inclusive character of the prayer is enhanced by the words 'at all times in all ways'. Peaceful relations within the congregation belong of course to the encompassing peace 'Paul' prays for. The help of the Lord in heaven strengthens the efforts of his congregation on earth.

The author adds a blessing to the prayer: 'The Lord be with you all'. It anticipates the standard blessing found in 3.18. Various liturgical formulae are heaped up in 3.16, 18; the result is marked by the repetition of 'all'.

3.17–18: THE LETTER-CLOSING

When we studied the pattern of ancient letters (see pp. 17–18), we saw that when the sender was not the actual, physical writer of the letter, the farewell could be added by the sender's own hand. We also saw, when we discussed 3.17 in connection with the question of the authorship of 2 Thessalonians, that Paul sometimes drew attention to such an addition by the phrasing used (1 Cor. 16.21; Gal. 6.11; Col. 4.18; Philem. 19), and that he probably added a few words with his own hand to all his letters. This Pauline habit has been imitated in 2 Thessalonians 3.17–18. We may suppose that in the autograph of the Deuteropauline letter 2 Thessalonians, there was no difference in handwriting between the final lines and the rest of the letter, because from the very beginning the letter was presented as a (fictive) copy of a letter Paul once sent to the Christians of Thessalonica.

In **3.17**, 'Paul' imitates, in a way which is, as we saw, somewhat 'overdone', Paul's habit of indicating in words that he now takes the pen in his own hand: 'The greeting is in my own hand: Paul. It is a mark in every letter; this is how I write'. The verse (its beginning agrees literally with 1 Cor. 16.21 and Col. 4.18) serves to suggest the personal, authoritative presence of the apostle in the letter and its authenticity as an apostolic letter. According to 3.17, all letters of 'Paul' are marked by a greeting in the apostle's own handwriting; this is, as we saw, probably correct for Paul's own letters. The words 'this is how I write' refer, within the fiction of pseudonymity, to the peculiarities of Paul's handwriting; Paul himself speaks in Galatians 6.11 of the 'large letters' with which he writes.

The letter is closed in **3.18** with a blessing: 'The grace of our Lord Jesus Christ be with you all'. We have already observed that the 'grace and peace' from the prescript return, in a chiastic pattern, at the end of the letter: 'peace' in 3.16, 'grace' here in 3.18. 'Paul' assures his addressees of the favour of Christ, which is also the favour God has shown in Christ. The wording of the final blessing is more or less standardized in the Pauline and Deuteropauline epistles (see, e.g., Rom. 16.20; Phil. 4.23). 2 Thessalonians 3.18 is almost identical to 1 Thessalonians 5.28, which is its probable source; our author added 'all', quite in line with his emphasis in 3.16. It is his final attempt to reinforce the cohesion of a community threatened by persecution and dissidence.

Conclusion: 2 Thessalonians and Paul

At the end of the chapter on the author of 2 Thessalonians, and in the commentary on 2 Thessalonians 2.15, we observed that the person who wrote this letter considered it as an authentic reinterpretation of 1 Thessalonians in a new situation. We have seen in the commentary how our author dealt with 1 Thessalonians and with other elements from Paul's heritage. We now turn to the question: was the author of 2 Thessalonians right in placing himself within the Pauline tradition, particularly as far as 1 Thessalonians is concerned?

In searching for an answer, we should try to be fair to him. We should beware of playing his letter off against 1 Thessalonians and the other authentic Pauline letters, by denigrating 2 Thessalonians and idealizing Paul's letters. We should also take into account that our author has written a relatively short letter, intended to address the specific problem posed by the conviction that the day of the Lord has arrived and by its practical consequences; in other words, his letter should not be assessed as if it pretended to present a complete theology.

The author of 2 Thessalonians is regularly reproached with an interest in future salvation at the expense of an interest in present salvation (so, e.g., the commentaries of Trilling 1980 and Marxsen 1982). In Paul's view, so it is said, God has realized in the death and the resurrection of Christ eschatological salvation as a present reality in which the believer is already partaking, and which will be consummated in the future; Paul puts his ethical imperatives on the basis of the indicative of salvation (see, e.g., 1 Thess. 5.1–11; Rom. 5.1–11; 6.1–14; 1 Cor. 6.9–20). It is then asserted that in 2 Thessalonians, on the other hand, Jesus' death and resurrection are not mentioned, that salvation belongs exclusively to the future, and that ethical imperatives are thus not founded on the indicative of present salvation.

Such a simple opposition, however, does not quite do justice to our author. It is true that he does not mention Jesus' death and resurrection, but his interest in Jesus as the exalted Lord who will return from heaven (see esp. 1.7; 2.8) evidently presupposes belief in Jesus' resurrection (cf. Jewett 1986: 26; Hartman 1990: 479): Jesus can only return from heaven as the Lord if he is now in heaven as the Lord, and he can only be now in heaven as the Lord if God raised him from among the dead and made him Lord (cf. Acts 2.36; Phil. 2.9–11). Jesus' resurrection in turn presupposes his death; implicit references to Jesus' death on the cross, as an act of his and God's love, are found in 2 Thessalonians 2.13, 16 (see the commentary above). We should also observe that our author's interest in the future is dominant but not exclusive. The community is 'in God our Father and the Lord Jesus Christ' (1.1), and they share in grace and peace from God and Christ (1.2, 12; 2.16; 3.16, 18). In the present, God is working in them through the Spirit (1.11; 2.13, 16–17; 3.3–5), and as it seems, they are already participating in Christ's glory (1.12; see the commentary). It is quite clear from 2.13–15 that the imperatives 'stand firm and hold fast' are a conclusion from the preceding description of what God has done for the believers (note 'so then' at the beginning of 2.15). The alternation of imperatives with statements of thanksgiving, prayer and trust in 2.13–3.5 also betrays resemblance to Paul's view of the relation between indicative and imperative.

Apparently, the author of 2 Thessalonians moves within the Pauline tradition. There are, however, also clear differences between him and Paul. The way in which he makes Paul's behaviour *per se* into an example to be imitated, omitting its motives (3.7–10), has no parallel in Paul's own letters. The same applies to his christology, in which the Lord Jesus Christ and God the Father are almost (but not quite) interchangeable.

Comparing 1 and 2 Thessalonians, we can only say that the author of 2 Thessalonians was correct in denying his opponents the right to appeal to 1 Thessalonians for the assertion that the Lord has already returned. There is, in 1 Thessalonians, a clear interest on the part of Paul in the parousia of Christ and in future salvation (see in 1 Thess. 1.10; 2.12, 19; 3.13; 4.14–17; 5.1–11). A statement such as 'you are all children of the light and children of the day' (1 Thess. 5.5) can only be read as implying that 'the day of the Lord has come' (2 Thess. 2.2) by thoroughly ignoring the context in which Paul has put it. On the other hand, it is quite clear in 1 Thessalonians that Paul expects the parousia to take place very soon, still during his own lifetime (4.15, 17), and, as said above, the opponents of our author may have asserted that the parousia Paul had thought to be imminent, had now indeed taken place. The author of 2 Thessalonians makes this appeal to 1 Thessalonians impossible not by in any way denying Paul's words, but by inserting certain events before the parousia. He neither confirms nor denies that the parousia will happen soon, although he seems to think that the end is near (2.7); he only completes, from his apocalyptic eschatology, what had, in his view, still been omitted by Paul. His completion cannot be said to be at variance with Paul's statement that he does not have to write to the Thessalonians about 'times and seasons', because they 'know that the day of the Lord comes like a thief in the night' (1 Thess. 5.1-2). In apocalyptic eschatology, one reckons on the one hand with a chain of events leading up to the end, and on the other with the impossibility for humans to know when God will bring about the end of the present age (see, e.g., Mark 13.28-37).

In spite of the presence of Pauline features in 2 Thessalonians, the letter is in fact made distinct from Paul's letters by its very strong, one-sided interest in the future; we should consider though that this one-sidedness is due to the situation in which the letter has been written (just as Paul's one-sidedness in Galatians is due to historical circumstances). The main concern of our author is to refute the conviction that the day of the Lord has already arrived. The congregation he addresses suffers persecution, and some of its members have tried to calm their distress by declaring that the parousia of Christ had occurred and by behaving accordingly. In this situation, the author of 2 Thessalonians urges his congregation to face the end with a sense of sobriety. They know that apostasy and the coming of the lawless one have to precede the parousia; these events have not yet taken place, because they are still restrained by God, who is the Lord of history, and it is thus impossible that the parousia has already occurred. The sense of sobriety implies a keen eye for the reality of evil: 'the mystery of lawlessness is already at work' (2.7) in persecution and oppression, and it also threatens the community from within through wrong ideas and wrong be-haviour. The readers have to be prepared for an increase of present evil up to the horrible acts of the lawless one and the apostasy brought about by him, but even the time of the final revelation of evil is determined by God.

At the same time, it is obvious that our author wishes to keep alive in his readers the expectation of Christ's parousia. In the first chapter of his letter, he shows that their sufferings are not meaningless, but that they are 'a token of God's just judgment' (1.5): when Christ returns, he will do justice to oppressors and oppressed. In the second chapter, he reminds them of the coming of the lawless one, to add immediately that 'the Lord Jesus will kill (him) with the breath of his mouth and destroy (him) by the manifestation of his coming' (2.8). The congregation has to live in the tension between hope and realism, between future and present. They are (as a community, not just each individual member) exhorted to endure the present distress, knowing that they are living at the threshold of the events of the end and that the decisions they make in the present will have a bearing on their future fate.

The author of 2 Thessalonians (and his original addressees) interprets history in terms of apocalyptic eschatology. The language and the imagery of apocalyptic eschatology are probably not immediately understood by most modern readers. Nevertheless, some understanding of them and of the underlying motives is essential for an insight into early Christian thought. We cannot simply repeat in our time a language and an imagery that are at home at the beginning of our era, but we can try to understand it as part of the communication between an author and the original addressees in a specific situation. We can then discover certain basic convictions in the Christian apocalyptic eschatology of a writing such as 2 Thessalonians: that history has a goal; that evil is a reality that should not be underestimated (an aspect often expressed in apocalyptic thought by means of personification); that the God who has revealed himself in Jesus governs history; that God and Jesus will not abandon those faithful to them; that justice will finally reign. The exhortation to face the end with sobriety may then even appeal to us.

Bibliography

Abbreviations

BETL	Bibliotheca Ephemeridum Theologicarum Lovaniensium
FFNT	Foundations and Facets: New Testament
JBL	*Journal of Biblical Literature*
LCL	Loeb Classical Library
NovT	*Novum Testamentum*
NTS	*New Testament Studies*
SBL	Society of Biblical Literature
TU	Texte und Untersuchungen
ZNW	*Zeitschrift für die neutestamentliche Wissenschaft*

Agrell, G. (1976) *Work, Toil and Sustenance. An Examination of the View of Work in the New Testament, Taking into Consideration Views Found in Old Testament, Intertestamental, and Early Rabbinic Writings*, Lund: Ohlssons.

Aus, R. D. (1973) 'The liturgical background of the necessity and propriety of giving thanks according to 2 Thess 1:3', *JBL* 92: 432–8.

—— (1976) 'The relevance of Isaiah 66.7 to Revelation 12 and 2 Thessalonians 1', *ZNW* 67: 252–68.

—— (1977) 'God's plan and God's power: Isaiah 66 and the restraining factors of 2 Thess 2:6–7', *JBL* 96: 537–53.

Barnouin, M. (1977) 'Les problèmes de traduction concernant II Thess. ii. 6–7', *NTS* 23: 482–98.

Bassler, J. M. (1984) 'The enigmatic sign: 2 Thessalonians 1:5', *Catholic Biblical Quarterly* 46: 496–510.

Beale, G. K. (1988) 'Revelation', in D. A. Carson and H. G. M. Williamson (eds), *It is Written: Scripture Citing Scripture. FS. B.*

Lindars, Cambridge: Cambridge University Press, pp. 318–36.

Best, E. (1972) *A Commentary on the First and Second Epistles to the Thessalonians* (Black's New Testament Commentaries), London: Black.

Betz, H. D. (1979) *Galatians. A Commentary on Paul's Letter to the Churches in Galatia* (Hermeneia), Philadelphia: Fortress Press.

Charlesworth, J. H. (ed.) (1983) *The Old Testament Pseudepigrapha, vol. 1: Apocalyptic Literature and Testaments*, London: Darton, Longman & Todd.

—— (1985) *The Old Testament Pseudepigrapha, vol. 2: Expansions of the 'Old Testament' and Legends, Wisdom and Philosophical Literature, Prayers, Psalms, and Odes, Fragments of Lost Judeo-Hellenistic Works*, London: Darton, Longman & Todd.

Collins, J. J. (1984) *The Apocalyptic Imagination. An Introduction to the Jewish Matrix of Christianity*, New York: Crossroad.

Collins, R. F. (1990) '"The gospel of our Lord Jesus" (2 Thes 1,8). A symbolic shift of paradigm', in R. F. Collins (ed.), *The Thessalonian Correspondence* (BETL 87), Leuven: Leuven University Press – Peeters, pp. 426–40.

Colson, F. H. and Whitaker, G. H. (1929–62) *Philo, with an English Translation*, 10 vols (LCL), Cambridge, MA: Harvard University Press/London: Heinemann.

Deissmann, A. (1923) *Licht vom Osten. Das Neue Testament und die neuentdeckten Texte der hellenistisch-römischen Welt*, 4th edn, Tübingen: Mohr.

Dibelius, M. (1937) *An die Thessalonicher I – II. An die Philipper* (Handbuch zum Neuen Testament 11), 3rd edn, Tübingen: Mohr.

Dobschütz, E. von (1909) *Die Thessalonicher-Briefe* (Meyers kritisch-exegetischer Kommentar über das Neue Testament), Göttingen: Vandenhoeck & Ruprecht.

Doty, W. G. (1973) *Letters in Primitive Christianity* (Guides to Biblical Scholarship), Philadelphia: Fortress Press.

Frame, J. E. (1912) *A Critical and Exegetical Commentary on the Epistles of St. Paul to the Thessalonians* (The International Critical Commentary), Edinburgh: T. & T. Clark.

Giblin, C. H. (1967) *The Threat to Faith. An Exegetical and Theological Re-examination of 2 Thessalonians 2* (Analecta Biblica 31), Rome: Pontifical Biblical Institute.

—— (1990), '2 Thessalonians 2 re-read as pseudepigraphal: a revised reaffirmation of *The Threat to Faith*', in R. F. Collins (ed.),

The Thessalonian Correspondence (BETL 87), Leuven: Leuven University Press – Peeters, pp. 459–69.

Grollenberg, L. (1978) *Paul*, trans. J. Bowden, London: SCM Press/ Philadelphia: Westminster Press.

Hartman, L. (1966) *Prophecy Interpreted. The Formation of Some Jewish Apocalyptic Texts and of the Eschatological Discourse Mark 13 par.* (Coniectanea biblica, New Testament 1), Lund: Gleerup.

—— (1990) 'The eschatology of 2 Thessalonians as included in a communication', in R. F. Collins (ed.), *The Thessalonian Correspondence* (BETL 87), Leuven: Leuven University Press – Peeters, pp. 470–85.

Holland, G. S. (1988) *The Tradition that You Received from Us: 2 Thessalonians in the Pauline Tradition* (Hermeneutische Untersuchungen zur Theologie 24), Tübingen: Mohr.

—— (1990) '"A letter supposedly from us": a contribution to the discussion about the authorship of 2 Thessalonians', in R. F. Collins (ed.), *The Thessalonian Correspondence* (BETL 87), Leuven: Leuven University Press – Peeters, pp. 394–402.

Hughes, F. W. (1989) *Early Christian Rhetoric and 2 Thessalonians* (Journal for the Study of the New Testament, Supplement Series 30), Sheffield: JSOT Press.

Jenks, G. C. (1991) *The Origins and Early Development of the Antichrist Myth* (Beihefte zur ZNW 59), Berlin: de Gruyter.

Jewett, R. (1986) *The Thessalonian Correspondence. Pauline Rhetoric and Millenarian Piety* (FFNT), Philadelphia: Fortress Press.

Jonge, M. de (1991) *Jesus, the Servant-Messiah*, New Haven: Yale University Press.

Kennedy, G. A. (1984) *New Testament Interpretation through Rhetorical Criticism* (Studies in Religion), Chapel Hill: University of North Carolina Press.

Koester, H. (1990) 'From Paul's eschatology to the apocalyptic schemata of 2 Thessalonians', in R. F. Collins (ed.), *The Thessalonian Correspondence* (BETL 87), Leuven: Leuven University Press – Peeters, pp. 441–58.

Koskenniemi, H. (1956) *Studien zur Idee und Phraseologie des griechischen Briefes bis 400 n. Chr.* (Annales Academiae Scientiarum Fennicae B 102/2), Helsinki: Suomalainen Tiedeakatemia.

Laub, F. (1973) *Eschatologische Verkündigung und Lebensgestaltung nach Paulus. Eine Untersuchung zum Wirken des Apostels beim Aufbau der Gemeinde in Thessalonike* (Biblische Untersuchungen 10), Regensburg: Pustet.

—— (1990) 'Paulinische Autorität in nachpaulinischer Zeit', in R. F. Collins (ed.), *The Thessalonian Correspondence* (BETL 87), Leuven: Leuven University Press – Peeters, pp. 403–17.

Lindemann, A. (1977) 'Zum Abfassungszweck des Zweiten Thessalonicherbriefes', *ZNW* 68: 35–47.

Malherbe, A. J. (1988) *Ancient Epistolary Theorists* (SBL Sources for Biblical Study 19), Atlanta, GA: Scholars Press.

Marxsen, W. (1982) *Der zweite Thessalonicherbrief* (Zürcher Bibelkommentare 11,2), Zürich: Theologischer Verlag Zürich.

Masson, Ch. (1957) *Les deux épîtres de saint Paul aux Thessaloniciens* (Commentaire du Nouveau Testament 11a), Neuchâtel – Paris: Delachaux & Niestlé.

Meade, D. G. (1986) *Pseudonymity and Canon. An Investigation into the Relationship of Authorship and Authority in Jewish and Early Christian Tradition* (Wissenschaftliche Untersuchungen zum Neuen Testament 39), Tübingen: Mohr.

Menken, M. J. J. (1985) *Numerical Literary Techniques in John. The Fourth Evangelist's Use of Numbers of Words and Syllables* (Supplements to NovT 55), Leiden: Brill.

Müller, P. (1988) *Anfänge der Paulusschule. Dargestellt am zweiten Thessalonicherbrief und am Kolosserbrief* (Abhandlungen zur Theologie des Alten und Neuen Testaments 74), Zürich: Theologischer Verlag.

Perry, B. E. (1965) *Babrius and Phaedrus* (LCL), Cambridge, MA: Harvard University Press/London: Heinemann.

Rigaux, B. (1956) *Saint Paul. Les épîtres aux Thessaloniciens* (Études Bibliques), Paris: Gabalda/Gembloux: Duculot.

Romaniuk, K. (1993) 'Les Thessaloniciens étaient-ils des paresseux?', *Ephemerides Theologicae Lovanienses* 69: 142–5.

Roosen, A. (1971) *De brieven van Paulus aan de Tessalonicenzen* (Het Nieuwe Testament), Roermond: Romen.

Rowland, C. (1982) *The Open Heaven. A Study of Apocalyptic in Judaism and Early Christianity*, London: SPCK.

Russell, R. (1988) 'The idle in 2 Thess 3.6–12: an eschatological or a social problem?', *NTS* 34: 105–19.

Schmidt, D. D. (1990) 'The syntactical style of 2 Thessalonians: How Pauline is it?', in R. F. Collins (ed.), *The Thessalonian Correspondence* (BETL 87), Leuven: Leuven University Press – Peeters, pp. 382–93.

Schmithals, W. (1965) *Paulus und die Gnostiker. Untersuchungen zu den kleinen Paulusbriefen* (Theologische Forschung 35), Hamburg-Bergstedt: Reich.

Schnider, F. and Stenger, W. (1987) *Studien zum neutestamentlichen Briefformular* (New Testament Tools and Studies 11), Leiden: Brill.

Schubert, P. (1939) *Form and Function of the Pauline Thanksgivings* (Beihefte zur *ZNW* 20), Berlin: Töpelmann.

Smit, J. (1989) 'The Letter of Paul to the Galatians: a deliberative speech', *NTS* 35: 1–26.

Smit Sibinga, J. (1986) 'Zur Kompositionstechnik des Lukas in Lk. 15:11–32', in J. W. van Henten a.o. (eds), *Tradition and Re-Interpretation in Jewish and Early Christian Literature. FS. J. C. H. Lebram* (Studia Post-Biblica 36), Leiden: Brill, pp. 97–113.

—— (1992) 'Towards understanding the composition of John 20', in F. Van Segbroeck a.o. (eds), *The Four Gospels 1992. FS. F. Neirynck* (BETL 100), Leuven: Leuven University Press – Peeters, pp. 2139–52.

Spicq, C. (1956) 'Les Thessaloniciens "inquiets" étaient-ils des paresseux?', *Studia Theologica* 10: 1–14.

Stephenson, A. M. G. (1968) 'On the meaning of *enestēken hē hēmera tou kuriou* in 2 Thessalonians 2,2', in F. L. Cross (ed.), *Studia Evangelica 4* (TU 102), Berlin: Akademie Verlag, pp. 442–51.

Stowers, S. K. (1986) *Letter Writing in Greco-Roman Antiquity* (Library of Early Christianity), Philadelphia: Westminster Press.

Strobel, A. (1961) *Untersuchungen zum eschatologischen Verzögerungsproblem, auf Grund der spätjüdisch-urchristlichen Geschichte von Habakuk 2,2 ff.* (Supplements to *NovT* 2), Leiden: Brill.

Sumney, J. L. (1990) 'The bearing of a Pauline rhetorical pattern on the integrity of 2 Thessalonians', *ZNW* 81: 192–204.

Taatz, I. (1991) *Frühjüdische Briefe. Die paulinischen Briefe im Rahmen der offiziellen religiösen Briefe des Frühjudentums* (Novum Testamentum et Orbis Antiquus 16), Freiburg Schw.: Universitätsverlag/Göttingen: Vandenhoeck & Ruprecht.

Thackeray, H. St J., Marcus, R., Wikgren, A. and Feldman, L. H. (1926–65) *Josephus, with an English Translation*, 9 vols (LCL), Cambridge, MA: Harvard University Press/London: Heinemann.

Trilling, W. (1972) *Untersuchungen zum 2. Thessalonicherbrief* (Erfurter Theologische Studien 27), Leipzig: St Benno Verlag.

—— (1980) *Der zweite Brief an die Thessalonicher* (Evangelisch-

Katholischer Kommentar zum Neuen Testament 14), Zürich: Benziger Verlag/Neukirchen-Vluyn: Neukirchener Verlag.

—— (1987) 'Die beiden Briefe des Apostels Paulus an die Thessalonicher. Eine Forschungsübersicht', in W. Haase and H. Temporini (eds), *Aufstieg und Niedergang der römischen Welt* II, 25.4, Berlin/New York: de Gruyter, pp. 3365–403.

Vermes, G. (1975) *The Dead Sea Scrolls in English*, Harmondsworth: Penguin.

Wanamaker, Ch. A. (1990) *The Epistles to the Thessalonians* (New International Greek Testament Commentary), Grand Rapids: Eerdmans/Exeter: Paternoster Press.

White, J. L. (1972) *The Form and Function of the Body of the Greek Letter. A Study of the Letter-Body in the Non-Literary Papyri and in Paul the Apostle* (SBL Dissertation Series 2), Missoula, MT: Scholars Press.

—— (1986) *Light from Ancient Letters* (FFNT), Philadelphia: Fortress Press.

Winter, B. W. (1989) '"If a man does not wish to work..." A cultural and historical setting for 2 Thessalonians 3:6–16', *Tyndale Bulletin* 40: 303–15.

Wrede, W. (1903) *Die Echtheit des zweiten Thessalonicherbriefs* (TU 9/2), Leipzig: Hinrichs'sche Buchhandlung.

Yarbro Collins, A. (1986) 'Introduction: Early Christian Apocalypticism', *Semeia* 36: 1–11.

Index of subjects

oppression *see* persecution and
oppression

Paradise 48, 138–41
parousia (second coming) of
Christ 1, 15, 23, 27, 28–9, 34,
35, 58, 59, 63, 71, 72, 76, 84–5,
87, 91, 114–15, 139, 143, 149;
Paul and 147–8; whether
already taken place 25, 96–101,
140–1
Paul 3, 4, 11–15, 16–19, 25–6, 65;
on road to Damascus 12, 57, *see
also* authorship of 2
Thessalonians
'Paul' (author of 2 Thessalonians)
63–4; example given by 73,
133–5; knowledge of letters of
Paul 78
peace 16, 18, 75, 77, 81, 143–4, 147
perdition, son of 71, 103–4, 113,
see also lawlessness, man of
persecution and oppression 64–5,
66, 70, 76, 77, 84–7, 89, 103,
126–7, 148–9
Petronius 106
Philemon 18
Philippi, church of 65
Philo of Alexandria 82
Phrygia 64
Picasso, Pablo, *Guernica* 45
place and date of 2 Thessalonians
64–6
pneuma 120–1
Polycarp, Bishop of Smyrna 11, 65
Pompey 105
prayer 70, 73, 75, 77, 123–4,
128–9, 143–4
prayer-report 75, 92–5
prescript 16, 25, 26, 27, 69, 75,
78–82, 144
Proclus 20
proem 17, 25, 26, 82, 86
prophets, false 59, 61, 100–1,
115–16
Pseudo-Demetrius 21
Pseudo-Phocylides 135
pseudonymity 40–3, 107, 122
punishment 88–9

Quintilius 21
Qumran community 46, 54, 84,
110, 112

reciprocity 125
reinterpretation 43
restraining power or person 29,
71, 72, 108–13
retribution 70, 76, 86–7
revelation 87–8, 91
Rhetoric Instruction (Quintilius) 21
rhetoric, three types of 21
Rhetoric to Herennius 21
rhetorical structure of letters 20–6
Rigaux, B. 25

saints 91
salvation 72, 81–2, 92, 118,
119–20, 121, 140, 143, 146
Satan 61, 111–12, 113, 115
Schmidt, D. D. 32
Schmidt, J. E. Chr. 28
second coming of Christ *see*
parousia
Seneca 11
signs and wonders 62, 115, 116
Silvanus (Silas) 11, 16, 27, 79–80,
87
Soviet Union 136
Spirit (*pneuma*) (of God or
human) 120–1
steadfastness 83–4, 129, 147
structure of 2 Thessalonians
69–78; numerical aspects 77–8
style of 2 Thessalonians 32–6, 43

Tammuz 104
Taxo 53–4
Tertullian 110
thanksgiving 69–70, 71–3, 77, 82,
119–21
theodicy 52, 53, 66, 89
Thessalonica, church of 2, 13, 15,
30, 42, 80
Timothy (Timotheus) 11, 16, 27,
31, 79, 80, 87, 134
Titus 134
tone of 2 Thessalonians 30–2, 43
Torah 52, 54, 83, 122

Index of references to biblical and other ancient literature

1 Old Testament

a Hebrew Old Testament

Genesis
1–3   130
3.14–19   131
3.16–19   139
3.17–19   131–4, 136, 138, 140–1
3.17   132
3.18   132
3.19   132, 134
5.24   46, 51
6.1–4   48

Exodus
3.2   88
7.3   115
19   56
21.23–5   86
23.20   127

Leviticus
11.44   121
18.4   131
18.5   52

Numbers
6.24–6   143
6.26   143
23–4   55
23.3   55
23.7   56
23.18   56
24.3–4   56

24.3   56
24.15–16   56
24.15   56
24.20   56
24.21   56
24.23   56

Deuteronomy
6.22   115
7.6–8   120
10.17–18   85
13.2–6   115
23.2–3   80
27.1   131
30.15–20   52
32.35   87, 89
33.1   55
33.2   55–6

1 Kings
11.14   115
22.23   117

2 Kings
4.8   134

Isaiah
1–66   41
2.6–22   90
2.6   90
2.10   90
2.11   91
2.17   91
2.19   90
2.20   91

13.6 118
15 58–9
15.1–5 122
15.1 17
15.3–5 19
15.20 8
15.22–53 29
15.23–8 59
15.23 8, 96, 99
15.24 114
15.26 114
15.51–5 59
15.52 99
16.10 80
16.13–14 141
16.15 8
16.21 35, 144
16.22 81

2 Corinthians
1.1 14, 18, 91
1.2 76, 79
1.3–11 124
1.3 17
1.8–11 126
1.12 83
1.19 80
2.15 117
3.18 94, 121
4.2 117
5.1–5 29
5.10 58, 81
5.14–15 120
5.17 128
6.2 120
6.7 117
9.2–3 83
10–12 20, 83
11.7–8 134
12.2–4 57
12.13 134
13.4 89
13.11 76, 125, 143
13.13 18, 76, 123

Galatians
1.1–5 16
1.1 16, 18, 123
1.2 80

1.3–4 82
1.3 76, 79
1.4 16, 59
1.5 19
1.6–7 17
1.11 17
1.13–17 12
1.13 80
1.14 122
1.15–16 57
2.2 126
2.5 117
2.14 117
2.20 120
3.13 61
4.6 80
4.20 13
5.1 122
5.5 84
5.7 117, 126
5.13–14 83
5.19–22 19
6.9 141
6.11 35, 144
6.16 76
6.17 125
6.18 76

Ephesians
1.1 18–9
1.2 76, 79
1.3 17
1.4–5 8, 120
3.1–19 42
4.28 136
6.10 125
6.19 125
6.23 76
6.24 76

Philippians
1.2 79
1.3–11 17
1.9 69
1.10 99
1.23 89
1.28 89
2.6–11 19, 81
2.9–11 81, 147